Doing It Our Way

The LTCB International Library Trust

The LTCB (Long-Term Credit Bank of Japan) International Library Trust, established in July 2000, is the successor to the LTCB International Library Foundation. It carries on the mission that the foundation's founders articulated as follows:

The world is moving steadily toward a borderless economy and deepening international interdependence. Amid economic globalization, Japan is developing ever-closer ties with nations worldwide through trade, through investment, and through manufacturing and other localized business operations.

Japan's global activity is drawing attention to its political, economic, and social systems and to the concepts and values that underlie those systems. But the supply of translations of Japanese books about those and other Japan-related subjects has not kept pace with demand.

The shortage of foreign-language translations of Japanese books about Japanese subjects is attributable largely to the high cost of translating and publishing. To address that issue, the LTCB International Library Foundation funds the translation and the distribution of selected Japanese works about Japan's politics, economy, society, and culture.

International House of Japan, Inc., manages the publishing activities of the LTCB International Library Trust, and Chuo Mitsui Trust and Banking Company, Ltd., manages the trust's financial assets.

LTCB International Library Selection No. 24

LTCB International Library Trust/International House of Japan

Doing It Our Way
A Sony Memoir

Norio Ohga
Translated by Brian Miller

This book was originally published in 2003 in a somewhat different form by the *Nihon Keizai Shimbun (Nikkei)* as *Sony no Senritsu*. International House of Japan retains the English-language translation rights under contract with Norio Ohga and through the courtesy of the *Nihon Keizai Shimbun*.

© 2008 International House of Japan

First English edition published March 2008 by International House of Japan
11-16, Roppongi 5-chome, Minato-ku, Tokyo 106-0032, Japan
Tel: +81-3-3470-9059   Fax: +81-3-3470-3170
E-mail: ihj@i-house.or.jp

Printed in Japan
ISBN 978-4-924971-25-7

Contents

Publisher's Note

This volume is an edited English translation of an autobiographical
book by Norio Ohga that appeared in 2003 as *Sony no Senritsu* (Sony
Melody). That book was an expanded version of a series of articles
that had appeared in Japan's leading business newspaper, the *Nihon
Keizai Shimbun* (*Nikkei*). The articles appeared in 2002 and 2003 in
the *Nikkei's* popular "Watashi no Rirekisho" (My C.V.) feature.

In preparing this English version, we have omitted material of interest primarily to Japanese readers, and we have added background
about subjects that might be unfamiliar to readers outside Japan. We
salute the *Nikkei's* Waichi Sekiguchi for his excellent work in editing
the Japanese texts that provided the basis for this book.

Ohga—professional musician, visionary executive, accomplished
pilot—ranks among Japan's most colorful business leaders of his generation. He presided over Sony's transformation from a purely manufacturing enterprise to a global leader in entertainment and games.
A towering figure in the history of a remarkable corporation, Ohga
personifies the globalization and digitization of Japanese industry.

This work spans the period from Ohga's years as a conservatory student and Sony recruit to his retirement from the presidency in 1995.
A great deal has happened at Sony, of course, in the past 13 years. But
the personal recollections on the following pages remain illuminating.
They furnish valuable insight into how Sony became what it is, and
they offer intriguing hints about the company's future direction.

Prelude

The Sony Pictures movie *Spider-Man* captured the imagination of American moviegoers as few movies ever have. *Godzilla*, released by Sony Pictures in 1998, was a big hit in its own right and helped restore the studio to financial sustainability. But *Spider-Man* was a cinematic phenomenon of historic proportions. Released in 2002, it was the movie that erased any remaining doubts about the value of the former Columbia Pictures Entertainment in Sony's business portfolio. *Spider-Man*, along with *Spider-Man 2* in 2004 and *Spider-Man 3* in 2007, filled theaters and sold innumerable DVDs, not to mention whetting untold appetites for DVD players.

Paying $4.8 billion for Columbia had struck numerous observers as reckless back in 1989. But that sum paled in comparison with the figures that would become commonplace in the sphere of corporate acquisitions. Sony's net worth is far more today than it was when the company acquired Columbia. The acquisition has more than justified management's belief in the potential for synergies between the tangibles of consumer electronics and the intangibles of entertainment media.

Moviemaking expanded Sony's well-established presence on the content side of the entertainment industry. That presence dated from the 1968 establishment of the joint venture CBS/Sony Records (now Sony Music Entertainment). It would grow even more prodigiously with the success of the PlayStation series of game consoles.

Sony's breathtaking advances in the entertainment business thus marked the first truly synergistic amalgam of digital tangibles and intangibles. But that is getting ahead of our story. Let us turn back the pages to an earlier era and discover in Sony's founders a pioneering awareness of the value of branding.

A four-letter word

"Maximize the brand value of the four letters of the Sony name." As the company's newly named president in 1982, that was how I answered journalists who asked about my management priorities. I had inherited the devotion to conscientious branding evoked memorably by Sony cofounder Akio Morita.

Prospective American partners recognized the potential value of the transistor radio that Morita took to the United States in 1955. But they warned him that it would never sell in the U.S. market under the still-unknown Sony brand. One company offered to place an order for 100,000 radios on the condition that the radios appear under that company's brand. Morita famously refused, insisting that the Sony brand would yet become a household name. His refusal set the tone for a corporate culture focused on building brand value.

Half a century later, a brand survey by the U.S. consultancy Landor Associates confirmed Sony's success in brand building. We ranked alongside such icons as Coca-Cola, Mercedes-Benz, and Kodak as one of the best recognized and most highly regarded brands on earth. Sony had become more than just a name on consumer electronics products and had acquired a ubiquitous visibility in popular culture.

Our company, which operated initially as Tokyo Tsushin Kogyo (Tokyo Telecommunications Engineering Corporation), changed its corporate name to Sony in 1958. Morita and the other executives had recognized the importance of unifying product and corporate branding to build a strong identity in world markets.

My first assignment on joining Sony in 1959 was as head of a production division responsible for developing and manufacturing broadcasting equipment, but my career soon took a fateful turn. I proposed to Morita shortly after coming aboard that we needed greater sophistication in our product designs and in our brand logo. He agreed heartily, and I promptly found myself in charge of the company's design office and advertising division. My career thereafter centered on work in asserting a unified design concept and building a strong brand. I remained involved in overseeing product design at Sony until being named president.

Capturing the imagination

Handsome, easily recognized logos for company names and trade-marks are important in branding. But corporate identity ultimately hinges on a company's ability to deliver products and services that capture the imagination of customers. Products that capture the imagination are goods that are appealing to the eye, that offer performance and quality that continue to delight, and that are altogether a pleasure to own. And our best guide in seeking to create such products is our own taste. We need to come up with the kinds of products that we ourselves would love to own and use. When we succeed, we can be reasonably confident that other consumers will also like the products.

Succeeding consistently in creating products that capture the imagination requires a systematic approach. Companies need to undertake coherent product planning and abide by well-established principles of industrial design. I overhauled Sony's approach to product design when I started at the company as the head of a production division. We established the distinctive two-tone combination of polished die-cast aluminum and matte black enamel. Our color scheme—dubbed simply "silver and black" at Sony—defined product design in consumer electronics for more than a generation and remains a powerful design motif in the industry.

In product planning, a three-year horizon proved useful with the products that we handled at Sony during my watch. We were always hard at work on new products for three years down the line. Having a hit product is exciting, but it's also distracting. You need to bear in mind the generally brief popularity of even the most successful products and keep focused on the next big thing.

Another requisite in product planning is to assert, whenever possible, a de facto standard. Microsoft's Windows operating system has become the byword for industry standards. But Sony has a long history of establishing industry standards. An early example was our work with Philips in positioning the cassette tape and the compact cassette tape recorder as a standard medium for audio equipment.

We also worked with Philips in developing compact disc (CD) technology and in positioning that technology as an industry standard. Digital media, we recognized, would be invaluable in allowing people to handle music and other content freely, and we were determined to secure a place in the vanguard of the digital revolution. We held a celebration in 2002 to mark the 20th anniversary of the sale of the first CD, and that was an occasion for marveling at the size of the market for CDs and at the spectacular range of applications that had emerged. The Recording Industry Association of America reported that Americans were purchasing some 900 million music CDs a year. And CD technology had become indispensable, of course, in personal computers and in game consoles, as well as in audio equipment.

Ten years after the debut of the CD, Sony launched the MiniDisc (MD) format. I oversaw the development of MD technology by a team of Sony engineers. The new technology multiplied the portability and convenience of CD technology immensely. It demonstrated the importance of following up even highly successful products with new-generation technologies.

Content and hardware

Driving Sony's growth has been a long-standing readiness—eagerness, even—to accompany business in physical products with ventures in intangible content, such as music, movies, and games. The proposals to acquire a music company and a movie company in the United States came from me, but Morita was totally supportive in each instance.

Sony seconded me in 1968 to the newly established CBS/Sony Records, a 50:50 joint venture with CBS Records. There, I supervised our successful diversification into the music business. The experience was invaluable in gaining the expertise and perspective that would serve us well in subsequent moves into the movie business and computer games. Sony acquired CBS Records in 1988, and the joint venture became the wholly owned subsidiary Sony Music Entertainment. The business meshed perfectly, of course, with our traditional and continually evolving product lines in audio equipment.

Our amalgamation of music hardware and content was thus an unqualified success from the beginning. Our moves in video hardware and content, though ultimately successful, had less-auspicious beginnings. We failed to establish our Betamax videocassette tape-recording format as a product standard in the consumer sector, though it became a standard format for professional video recording. And Columbia Pictures Entertainment was notoriously unprofitable in the first years after its 1989 acquisition by Sony. Our commitment to amalgamating content and hardware was unflagging, however, and perseverance ultimately yielded profitable synergies in movies, as well as in music.

The synergies were even more striking in computer game consoles and software. Our PlayStation series, launched in 1994, became the most successful consumer electronics product ever. We maintained the product's sales momentum with the widely hailed launches of the PlayStation 2 in 2000 and the PlayStation 3 in 2006. Customers around the world had purchased more than 100 million PlayStation consoles by the end of 2006. The PlayStation product line has become a source of ¥1 trillion (more than $8 billion) in annual revenue at Sony alone. Including third-party sales of game software, the PlayStation is a global industry worth nearly $20 billion in annual sales.

Laying a sound foundation

Sony's inroads into musical, cinematic, and game content heightened the importance of reinforcing its fiscal footing in more-traditional businesses. The entertainment business is notoriously volatile. Although our music, movie, and game operations became profitable overall, they remained inherently high-risk, high-return ventures. A huge hit like *Spider-Man* would earn a massive return on investment, but a box-office flop—and we certainly had our share of those—was money down the drain.

Business in electronic components has been especially valuable in steadying our earnings. Highly advanced, highly original components developed in-house underpin the competitiveness of our electronic products. Profitability in manufacturing, however, depends heavily on economies of scale. And Sony had traditionally manufactured components mainly for its own products, which limited those economies unnecessarily.

After becoming president, I steered the company into the business of marketing components actively to third-party customers. Sony cofounder Masaru Ibuka, an engineer, looked askance at my policy. But our new business in charge-coupled devices, batteries, and other components became a large and reliable source of sales and earnings, and the increased economies of scale reduced our unit costs greatly. The steady profitability of that business hedged our profitability against the earnings volatility of our fast-expanding business in entertainment content.

Frictions inevitably arose between the contrasting work ethics of our traditional electronics businesses and our content businesses, and harmonizing our diverse operations was a persistent challenge. The content business—movies, especially—entails huge production costs and lavish spending on promotion. In stark contrast to that flamboyance is the penny-pinching frugality of the manufacturer. The people in our manufacturing operations were understandably perturbed when our movie business was unprofitable and we were, in the eyes of some, throwing good money after bad. Blessed with superior management talent, we gradually succeeded in blending our operations into a harmonious and even synergistic whole. Everyone was grateful and relieved, meanwhile, when earnings from our increasingly profitable content business offset a slump in the electronics sector.

Sony's sales increased fourfold during my 13 years at the helm. That growth resulted from wholesale expansion into new markets, as well as from continuing gains in traditional lines of business. I frequently recalled the words of Ibuka in his founding prospectus for our company. He cautioned against seeking size for the sake of size, and I felt his stern gaze keenly as we expanded rapidly. Our growth, though, was genuinely organic—hardly a matter of seeking size for the sake of size. And we put in place a solid management framework to coordinate our expansion. I instituted a system of semiautonomous business groups in 1983, the year after I became president, and we realigned our operations anew in 1994 as eight in-house companies.

Our system of in-house companies was notably useful in accommodating the differences in corporate culture between our content businesses and our traditional manufacturing businesses. It was also useful in speeding decision making in all our operations. Each company was responsible for its business planning, including investment, and the head of each bore the title "president."

We took another important step in strengthening our management framework in 1997. Japanese corporate management had long differed fundamentally from the U.S. model in its approach to corporate governance. Directors at U.S. corporations were responsible for overseeing the performance of management, largely from the perspective of maximizing shareholder value. One or two members of the management team, such as the president and chief financial officer, might serve concurrently as board members, but for the most part U.S. companies maintained a clear division between the oversight function and the managerial function. In contrast, nearly all directors at Japanese corporations, including Sony, served concurrently as managers responsible for day-to-day business operations. That system had worked well in Japan, but it was increasingly unsuited to the demands of corporate governance in an era of globalization.

In 1997, Sony adopted a system that allocated managerial responsibility for the in-house companies to newly established officers and oversight responsibility to the directors. Several officers served as directors to maintain a close linkage between the oversight and managerial functions. So our new approach to corporate governance was something of a hybrid of traditional Japanese and U.S. practices. It provided an excellent foundation for continuing growth for Sony in the global markets of the 21st century.

Retaining a start-up mentality

Sony has managed to retain the venture-business vitality that animated the company in its earliest days as a corporate start-up. That lasting vitality is a tribute to Morita's consistent emphasis on emphasizing capability and performance over academic credentials and on localizing our approach to business in markets around the world.

Flexibility in human resources management has enabled Sony to attract highly capable and motivated individuals who were dissatisfied with their jobs at more-conservative companies. That same flexibility has energized our workforce by enabling young managers to advance as rapidly as their creativity and commitment justified. And blindness to nationality in hiring and promotions has enabled the company to attract multinational talent.

The passion evinced by cofounders Ibuka and Morita persuaded me to abandon a nascent career as an operatic baritone. Morita suggested that a career at Sony needn't oblige me to abandon music as a serious avocation. In fact, a career at Sony meant new challenges daily and a lifelong race across the face of the planet. Not until late in my career did I regain the time to devote myself anew to music—including the chance to try my hand at conducting. Decade after decade passed as if in the batting of an eye. But that is simply evidence of the continuing excitement that is Sony. I hope that this book will convey some of that excitement.

Innovation in combining technology with value-added content has long since become the chief driver of industrial and economic progress. The story of Sony is the tale of a pioneer in that kind of inventiveness. I am proud that Sony continued to reinvent itself during my years at the helm, and I am honored to have this opportunity to share that story with readers.

I

Encountering a Genius

Sony entered my life in 1948, a year before I entered the Tokyo National University of Fine Arts and Music. Masaru Ibuka and Akio Morita had launched the company, initially called Tokyo Tsushin Kogyo (Tokyo Telecommunications Engineering Corporation), in May 1946. Ibuka came to my hometown to seek investment from a local businessman who was a friend and neighbor of my family. The company, Ibuka confided, was on the verge of producing Japan's first-ever tape recorder, and it needed a capital infusion to fund the project. Our family friend was impressed and told me that I should meet Ibuka. Although I was just a high school student, I jumped at the earliest chance to visit the new company in Tokyo.

Ibuka and Morita had met in the navy during the war. Their founding workplace was in space rented from a department store in Tokyo's Nihombashi district. By the time of my visit, they had moved a

Ibuka (left) and Morita, several years after founding their company

couple miles south. They wanted to have a factory of their own and had purchased and refitted a rough-hewn building formerly used by a carburetor manufacturer as an employee cafeteria. That was in the Gotenyama district, where Sony still maintains its global headquarters. People seemed happy with the new quarters. They finally had a workplace, some of them told me, big enough to accommodate everyone at the same time.

The factory was a decidedly unimpressive structure, however, and the thought of working at such a place never entered my mind, notwithstanding Ibuka's considerable appeal as an engineer and as a person. My next encounter with Ibuka was after I entered the Tokyo National University of Fine Arts and Music. Tokyo Tsushin Kogyo had put its tape recorder—the Tapecorder Model G—into production, and a salesman from the company was pitching the new product to the university.

I was the one who had piqued people's interest in tape recorders on the campus. Having read up on the new technology in foreign magazines, I became convinced that it was indispensable. "The tape recorder is for a musician," I argued, "what the mirror is for a ballerina." At my urging, the university secured funding from the Ministry of Education [now the Ministry of Education, Culture, Sports, Science and Technology] to make the purchase.

Tokyo Tsushin Kogyo's salesman left a tape recorder with the university to evaluate. Several shortcomings were immediately apparent. I drew up a list of about 10 serious problems with the machine and told the salesman that the university would not buy one until his company had resolved the problems. My memo, I learned later, set off a furor at the factory. It occasioned a summons for my second visit to Tokyo Tsushin Kogyo. I held my ground in a discussion with the factory manager about the technical specifications of the microphone, and he wondered aloud how a college student could know so much about tape recorders.

Ibuka took an interest in the cheeky but surprisingly knowledgeable university student and began inviting me to dinner. He was old

Tokyo Tsushin Kogyo's headquarters in Tokyo's Gotenyama district

enough to be my father, but we were kindred spirits. Ibuka had been an amateur radio buff in high school, and he earned a reputation at Tokyo's Waseda University as an inventive genius. My host would nod in agreement as I related the latest news from abroad about advances in recording technology. Neither of us liked alcohol. Our shared love of the new technology was our intoxicant, and we always had lots to talk about.

I was earning good money through singing work at a radio station in Tokyo, and in my third year at university I began entertaining thoughts of continuing my studies in Germany after graduation. The notion of polishing my art in the land of Beethoven and other titans of classical music was simply irresistible.

When graduation day arrived, Ibuka dispatched a car to pick me up after the ceremony and take me to Tokyo Tsushin Kogyo head-quarters. Awaiting me there were Ibuka and Morita, and the two promptly asked me to sign on with the company as a contract employee. I protested that I was about to leave for Germany, but they persisted. All I needed to do, they explained, was send occasional reports about technological developments in Europe. The monthly stipend, they added, would surely come in handy.

Getting to Germany

I stayed on at the Tokyo National University of Fine Arts and Music for a year of graduate study before embarking for Germany. When the time came to leave, the choice of transport options loomed: by air or by sea. The sea voyage took about a month. Flying—in a propeller airliner—took about 48 hours. The fare for either option was about ¥200,000. That was a king's ransom in an era when lots of Japanese subsisted on a monthly income of only around ¥3,000.

Only three graduates of the Tokyo National University of Fine Arts and Music traveled to Europe to study that year, and we were keenly aware of our good fortune. One of us, a pianist by the name of Midori Matsubara, was bound for the Vienna University of Music and Performing Arts. Midori—who would later become my wife—took a plane to arrive in time for the entrance audition. I was more than happy to travel at a more leisurely pace and enjoy the sites along the way, and I therefore secured passage on a cargo-passenger liner. Joining me on the ship was the third Europe-bound musician, Sumiko Iuchi, whose boyfriend was awaiting her in Europe.

Our transport, the *Meirinsan-maru*, was debarking on its maiden voyage. The original itinerary provided for a departure from Yokohama, which is adjacent to Tokyo. That changed to a port in my home prefecture of Shizuoka to allow for loading a cargo of tea, so we began our journey with a train ride to the port city of Shimizu. No sooner had we boarded ship than a typhoon arose on our course and obliged the captain to wait out the storm in Kobe, and nearly a week passed before we finally left Japanese waters.

A former voice teacher of mine was studying in Munich, so I opted to begin my German sojourn there. I finally arrived in Munich in late October, fully six weeks after we set sail from Shimizu. The extended voyage suited me fine. I'd visit the bridge, and the captain and the other officers would show me how to measure the angle of the sun with a sextant and how to chart our course. By the time we had passed through the Suez Canal and docked in the northern Italian port of Genoa, I had received a crash course in navigation. The knowledge gained on that voyage served me well later in life when I earned a small-craft license.

Munich's musical Japanese contingent turned out in force to meet me at the train station. I settled into my studies there and had become acclimated when I decided that I really ought to see Berlin. The Easter holidays provided the opportunity for a visit. Japan's Michiko Tanaka was apparently a respected vocalist in Berlin, and I took in hand a written introduction to her from the former provost of a leading Japanese conservatory. When I called from the airport, she instructed me to come directly to her house, adding, "I'll have a meal ready for you."

Under the wing of Michiko Tanaka

"Ohga is the name of a Japanese diplomat here whom I absolutely despise." Those were the first words I heard from Michiko Tanaka on arriving at her home. The villain, I learned, had run off with a young female Japanese violinist nominally under the care of Tanaka. Then: "You seem to be of a different sort," she conceded on looking me carefully in the eye. "Why don't you come around once in a while."

Tanaka, divorced from a wealthy European industrialist, had married the stunningly handsome German actor Victor de Kowa. The couple occupied a palace-like mansion on the outskirts of Berlin. She was a disarmingly down-to-earth woman who delighted in looking out for Japanese students in the city. Her husband was a hugely talented and justly acclaimed star, and I benefited repeatedly from his generosity and goodwill.

On Tanaka's advice, I left the university where I was studying in Munich after a year and transferred to the Berlin University of the Arts. That was before the erection of the Berlin Wall, and the grandeur of the historic capital assured me that I had been right in switching venues. Tanaka called one day to invite me to come with her to the Savoy Hotel to "meet someone interesting." I knew enough to take the woman at her word, and the "someone interesting" turned out to be the newly appointed conductor of the Berlin Philharmonic, Herbert von Karajan. He had moved to Berlin in 1955 as Wilhelm Furtwängler's successor on the podium there.

As a conservatory student in Berlin

Karajan had found sanctuary at the de Kowa-Tanaka home during the chaos that preceded the fall of Berlin. The couple had opened their doors to numerous individuals who had become targets of Nazi persecution. Karajan was a member of the Nazi Party, but he had married a woman in 1942 whose grandfather was Jewish, and that compromised his standing with the Nazis. His lasting gratitude toward Tanaka was readily apparent.

A quarter century later, Karajan participated wholeheartedly in developing the specifications for compact disc technology, and that became an opportunity for me to get to know him extremely well. I had been so nervous at my first encounter with the legendary conductor that I could hardly speak. We shared a hearty laugh at the memory after I revealed that the petrified student with Tanaka at the Savoy Hotel had been me.

Performing The Telephone

Another memory of Berlin is the staging of Gian Carlo Menotti's opera *The Telephone*. I performed in the role of the male lead, and a Dutch student was the female lead. The opera centers almost exclusively on the interplay between the two leads, but my counterpart was extremely cold to me throughout the rehearsals. She finally explained to me that her father had been killed by Japanese troops in view of her mother. The young singer eventually overcame her distaste for Japanese and even welcomed me and some other students from Japan at her home in the Netherlands.

A visit by Soichiro Honda

Something that had struck me on arriving in Germany was the vast differential between that nation and Japan in economic might and in standards of living. Japanese, I could see, faced an immense task. We would need to work a lot harder if our nation was to earn a respected place in the international community. A company that, along with Sony, came to symbolize the hard work and innovation that would drive Japan's economic resurgence was Honda. And I was awestruck when Honda's eponymous founder paid me a visit in Berlin.

The father of my bride to be was a prominent physician and medical school professor in Tokyo and a consulting physician to Honda Motor. He wrote me that Soichiro Honda and one of his senior executives would be making a business trip to Germany and asked me to assist them in any way possible during their stay. The assignment proved a joy, as the Honda founder and his colleague turned out to be utterly delightful companions.

"We're in your hands," declared the founder when we met. Patting me firmly on the back, he continued: "We don't know the language, don't know up from down here. We'll be grateful for anything you can do to smooth things along." The two were in Germany for a week to inspect the machine tools that Honda was purchasing for a new plant. I "smoothed things along," as requested, by interpreting for my guests and even by arranging their meals. We enjoyed each other's company immensely, and laughter cascaded through our time together. That was the beginning of a close and lasting camaraderie with the Honda founder.

Soichiro and his remarkable wife were cast from a different mold from the typical Japanese industrialists of the day. They enjoined their son, for example, from following his father into the family business. Avoiding the hex of nepotism was instrumental in Honda's growth and vitality. Soichiro, by the way, never showed his face in the office after retiring. He was determined not to interfere in the work of advancing the company that he had launched.

Working both sides of the fence

Honda's great rival in the motorcycle marketplace was Yamaha, and I happened to be friends, too, with the head of that company, Genichi Kawakami. Yamaha's headquarters was in my home prefecture of

Shizuoka. The company had built a big business in musical instruments, as well as in motorcycles, and Kawakami was responsible for the musical side of the business in Tokyo when I was at the Tokyo National University of Fine Arts and Music. He appeared on campus frequently, and we developed a close relationship that continued after he became president at Yamaha.

I turned to Kawakami for funding for a graduation trip that we were planning. He complied but attached the condition that we make the trip to Yamaha's hometown, Hamamatsu, and perform at a musical instruments plant for the employees. We got a grand tour of the plant and then gave a well-received performance for the employees. That evening, we enjoyed a sumptuous repast at a luxury inn and spent the night there, all courtesy of Yamaha. It appears to have been a wise investment for Kawakami, judging from the stream of orders for Yamaha pianos that later emanated from the students' families.

A brash comment that I made during our dinner in Hamamatsu had a riveting effect on Kawakami. I declared that the steel frames in Yamaha pianos were the most unsightly in the world. Kawakami insisted that I meet the next day with his engineers. He assembled his entire engineering team, and the cocksure college student explained that well-crafted, elegantly finished metal frames are absolutely essential to good pianos. I cited the exquisite frames in the pianos of the U.S. company Steinway, and I noted that Yamaha's frames compared poorly with even those of the company's smaller Japanese rival Kawai. Kawakami invited me back repeatedly to Hamamatsu to discuss issues that arose in his company's musical instruments business. He seemed genuinely disappointed on hearing, when I returned from Germany, that I had decided to join Sony.

Hosting another visitor from Japan

My graduation recital at the Berlin University of the Arts went well, and I graduated in July 1957 at the head of my class. Just as I was making preparations to return to Japan, a letter arrived from Morita. He reported that Ibuka was planning a trip to Germany and asked me to show the Sony cofounder around.

Ibuka was ostensibly coming to Germany to tour tape recorder factories. But once he had arrived, he was the very picture of apathy. Ibuka displayed no interest whatsoever, either at the Telefunken plant near Hamburg or the Grundig plant in Nuremberg. He instructed me indifferently to "ask some questions and write up something for the report."

Only when we reached a prominent manufacturer's Belgian plant that produced semiconductor materials did Ibuka finally come alive. His eyes fairly glowed as we toured the plant. Sony had begun manufacturing transistors while I was studying in Germany, and Ibuka's interest had shifted completely from tape recorders to semiconductors. When I got back to Japan, I mentioned to Morita my astonishment at the profound change in his partner. "Yes," acknowledged Morita with a wry smile, "he has a remarkable way of jumping headlong into the next big thing."

Morita was a fastidious correspondent, and I received more letters from him than from anyone else while I was in Germany. His handwriting, however, was atrocious, and Ibuka's was even worse. I took some illicit consolation in the only fault I could discern in the two geniuses.

Tying the knot

Little in the way of romantic interest had embellished my life as a student, either in Japan or in Germany. That was before Midori Matsubara and I discovered a special feeling for each other. Midori had rented a room from an elderly Viennese widow who was a splendid cook and who treated her young Japanese boarder like a daughter. We had exchanged a few letters, and we met in Vienna at the end of 1954, our first Christmas season in Europe. A Japanese friend who was working as a professor in Germany and I had decided to spend the holiday in Vienna, and Midori found lodging for us just a five-minute walk from where she was staying.

Vienna was exhilarating, and we enjoyed long walks together through the city. Midori and I were still "just friends," however, when we both attended a monthlong Wagner symposium in Bayreuth the following summer. We were two of just four Japanese participants in the symposium, which amounted to total immersion in Wagner's oeuvre. When not attending performances, we were observing the rehearsals. Midori and I came away from Bayreuth with a new sense

The author and his bride to be before Berlin's Brandenburg Gate

of mutual affinity, and our feelings deepened after she transferred to a university in Berlin. Her dedication to her musical studies was inspiring to witness, and I found myself thinking that, if I was to marry anyone, this was surely the right person.

Midori agreed to marry me, and I wrote her father to request his permission. My father had passed away when I was a fourth-year university student. Dr. Matsubara wrote back that we should discuss the subject after his daughter and I returned to Japan. He was favorably disposed to our getting married, however, and gave his formal blessing as soon as we got back to Japan in September 1957. The preparations for the wedding began immediately, and we held the ceremony less than two months later, on November 1.

Only later did I learn that Dr. Matsubara had wanted me to become his adopted son. That's a common practice in Japan when the bride has no brothers to inherit the family name. Midori was the oldest of four children, all female. She was adamantly opposed to her father's demand, however, and persuaded him to abandon the idea.

Our wedding took place in an elegant new hotel just across the moat from the Imperial Palace. Ibuka served in the symbolic role of go-between. I owed him and others at Sony more than ever, since Ibuka had provided me with airfare for the trip home. Morita was out of town on business, but his wife attended on his behalf.

II

Joining the Company

Midori and I settled into newlywed life in Tokyo in a house that her father built for us on family property. She went to work full time as the music supervisor at a kindergarten and elementary school. I joined a group that staged operas and other musical events throughout Japan and soon had a busy schedule as a soloist. Still beckoning, however, was the company that was growing rapidly under the leadership of Ibuka and Morita.

I remained on the Tokyo Tsushin Kogyo payroll in Japan as a contract employee, though my consulting duties were light and vaguely defined. The company had opened its first overseas office, in New York, in September 1957—the month that Midori and I returned home from Europe. Four months later, Tokyo Tsushin Kogyo became Sony, unifying its corporate identity and its increasingly visible product brand. The name change signaled a commitment to transcending the company's Japanese origins and stepping out onto the world stage. Sony reinforced its financial wherewithal for fulfilling that commitment by listing its shares on the Tokyo Stock Exchange in late 1958.

The Sony nomenclature first gained prominence as the name on pocket transistor radios sold in the United States. It was a combination of *sonus*, the Latin root of sound and sonic, and the more-ingratiating *sonny*. In Japan, Tokyo Tsushin Kogyo was becoming familiar as Totsuko, an abbreviation that comprised the first syllable of each word in its name. Management had the good sense and the foresight, however, to recognize that the ever-so-Japanese name would not resonate with consumers in other nations.

My agreement with Sony called for me to show up at headquarters once a week. I dutifully found time between concert engagements to fulfill that responsibility. The success of Sony's transistor radios and other products occasioned a flood of licensing inquiries and agreements, and my language skills and familiarity with foreign nations proved useful. I loved the atmosphere at the company, where something exciting was always happening, and I was soon stopping by the office twice and even three times a week.

What sealed my fate with Sony was a business trip on which I accompanied Morita to the United States and Europe in 1959. That was a time when American President Line, United States Line, and other operators of luxury passenger liners were vying for the fastest times across the Atlantic. I had fallen in love with sea travel on my cruise to Europe as a student, and I was determined that Morita and I should travel in style. We should fly to Europe, I suggested, but take a liner across the Atlantic to the United States and then fly home. Morita, a navy veteran, was fascinated at the thought of passenger ships as fast as a destroyer.

Morita and I made our way around Europe, and he signed contracts and took care of other business. We finally arrived in the southern U.K. port of Southampton to embark on our voyage to New York on the *S.S. United States*. The trip took five days. With little else to do, we passed much of the time in and around the swimming pool. The *S.S. United States* sped along at around 35 knots. Its brisk pace kept the water in the pool highly agitated and rendered swimming, per se, all but impossible.

We would swim as best we could for a while and then retire from the pool for our daily debate. The subject of the debate was inevitably Sony. I noted repeatedly that Sony's design was primitive and immature in comparison with the company's European and U.S. competitors. Morita replied that Sony needed someone alert to that difference to take charge of upgrading its design. The more I pointed out shortcomings in Sony's design and corporate branding, the more forcefully Morita insisted that I should come aboard.

Back in Tokyo, my wife and I received an invitation from the Moritas to an exclusive restaurant in Tokyo's Akasaka nightlife district. Morita and his wife directed all their charm and persuasiveness at me in making a convincing case for joining Sony. I was already 29 years old, noted Morita, and acquiring a well-rounded competence in management would take around 10 years. He insisted that the job would leave time for me to pursue musical pursuits. Morita cited a Japanese proverb about the value of keeping two pairs of sandals—a proverb roughly analogous to the English expression "wearing more than one hat." I wasn't so naive as to think that I could really maintain parallel careers, but Morita made it sound almost possible. Whatever I was thinking at the time, I agreed to go to work full time at Sony.

I had expressed a preference for a position in product development, and Morita initially put me in charge of a division that developed and manufactured tape recorders for radio stations. But as soon as I went to work, I began noticing lots of things that needed to be done. What bothered me most was the Sony logo, which had become ubiquitous since the company's name change. The typography was impossibly awkward.

Morita responded to my call for a new logo by putting me in charge of the design office. When I asked who would take over my tape recorder production division, he replied that Sony needed me there, too. My enthusiasm had earned me the dubious result of doubling my management responsibilities. I compounded my foolishness by suggesting changes in our advertising, which was horribly unsophisticated. That imprudent suggestion saddled me with the additional job of running the advertising division.

On tour

My broadening responsibilities at Sony left me with hardly enough time even to return home nightly. Musical activities away from the office were an increasingly tenuous proposition, but I was determined to continue my musical career. I improvidently accepted the role of the count in a new production of Mozart's *The Marriage of Figaro*.

The Kyoto Symphony Orchestra was the pit orchestra for the production, and its conductor, the German Carl Caelius, was the musical director. Kyoto was the venue for the initial performances, which went well and even earned a prestigious musical prize from the *Mainichi Shimbun* newspaper. On tap for 1960, however, was a nationwide tour for the opera, and I was becoming doubtful about my ability to perform operatically on the road while performing managerially at Sony. Events would prove my doubts well founded.

My worst fears materialized at our performance in Hiroshima. The performance happened to be on the day when Sony finalized a large

In costume for The Marriage of Figaro

sale of equipment to a Hiroshima broadcaster. We had negotiated long and hard to win the contract with the broadcaster, and my subordinates from Tokyo headed off after the signing to toast the triumph. Exhausted, I headed for the auditorium where we were staging the opera.

I put my fatigue aside and somehow negotiated the first three acts. The third act presents the most singing for the count, and the relief of getting through that act, combined with severe sleep deprivation, produced a near-disastrous result. I had changed costumes and was awaiting my entrance in the fourth act, which is essentially an extended finale. Drowsiness overcame me in that brief span. Leaning on a wardrobe trunk, I was fast asleep, slumbering contentedly to the strains of Mozart. A familiar melody jolted me awake. "My cue. I'm on!"

My entrance was properly from the left side of the stage, but I had fallen asleep on the right side. Time did not allow for me to work my way backstage to the correct position, so I boldly entered from the opposite side. The singers in the roles of Figaro and his betrothed, Susanna, had their backs to the audience at that juncture, and the two guffawed at my errant entrance. I dropped the first couple of lines, but the lapse went unnoticed to nearly everyone in the audience.

As soon as the curtain came down, I headed straight for Maestro Caelius to make my apology. He was wondrously forgiving and graciously expressed surprise that someone could serve in his cast while shouldering such taxing responsibilities elsewhere. Nonetheless, the experience was a wake-up call. I recognized that wearing the two hats of corporate manager and opera singer was becoming unfeasible.

My operatic colleagues encouraged me to persevere, and an unexpected opportunity persuaded me to extend my musical career one more concert. Japan's public broadcaster, NHK, was to stage Engelbert Humperdinck's opera *Hansel and Gretel* at 1960 year-end under the direction of the composer's son, Wolfram. The television director responsible for the production at NHK knew me well and asked me to take the role of Hansel and Gretel's father. I found the offer irresistible and accepted, but the engagement was to entail yet another conflict with my duties at Sony.

The first-ever strike by Sony's labor union erupted on the day of the dress rehearsal for the opera. Whereas the labor unions of North America and Europe tend to be vocation based and to span multiple companies, labor unions in Japan tend to be company based and to encompass nonmanagerial full-time employees of all job classifications. A picket line formed in front of our headquarters, and my responsibilities as a general manager precluded my leaving the building.

I called NHK and pleaded with the producer to stage the opera sans father. He responded predictably that such a staging change was out of the question. The producer went so far as to offer to dispatch a helicopter, if necessary, to fetch me to the dress rehearsal.

Ultimately, the strike ended in time for me to hold an individual dress rehearsal with the television director and the stage director. The performance series got under way the next day and proceeded without a hitch, earning critical acclaim. But my musical endeavors were interfering too much with my work at Sony, and the role in *Hansel and Gretel* was to be my last as a professional opera singer.

Two years later, I took the stage once more to conduct the Brahms *Requiem* with the Tokyo Philharmonic. A friend who had studied music in Germany when I was there had returned to Japan. He was to appear as the baritone soloist, and he implored me to conduct. No good deed goes unpunished, and the concert occasioned the inevitable conflict with my work at Sony. The time and date scheduled for the dress rehearsal coincided spectacularly with a meeting of the Sony board of directors—a meeting where I was to make an important presentation. That forced me to forego the dress rehearsal and plunge headlong into the performance. Fortunately, things went well, but the experience persuaded me once and for all to eschew any further musical activities in the public sphere.

III

Sony Design

The work at Sony that had obliged me to put my operatic career on ice became increasingly demanding. Placing me in charge of product design and advertising had integrated the company's brand-building functions. A review by the design office became an integral part of the approval process for every product design and for every advertisement.

Tweaking the Sony logo was my first big undertaking as the head of design. The figure on the following page presents a historical series of Sony logos. All four letters in the 1957 version are of the same type size, but the eye perceives the *S* as disproportionately small and the *Y* as disproportionately large. I resolved that problem by slightly enlarging the *S* and slightly shrinking the *Y* in the revised logo that appeared in 1961. That revision also included thickening the letters. People had noted that our big neon sign in Hong Kong was difficult to read in the fog, and the thicker letters improved readability greatly. Today's Sony

⬡ ─────────	Tokyo Tsushin Kogyo emblem
─────────	1955
SONY ─────────	1957
SONY ─────────	1961
SONY ─────────	1962
SONY ─────────	1969
SONY ─────────	1973

The evolution of the Sony logo

logo appeared in 1973 as the sixth revision after the emergence of the first Sony logo in 1955.

The requisites of global, long-term brand building mandated bold moves. That included doing away with a cute character that Sony had deployed for displays at its affiliated retailers in Japan. Endearing as the character was, it was inconsistent with the identity that we were seeking to build as a global corporation. Japanese disdain imposing decisions unilaterally, especially when the decisions are potentially discomfiting to a lot of people. So I personally visited the well-known cartoonist that Sony had commissioned to create the character to explain my reasoning. He rewarded my concern for his feelings by generously expressing full understanding of the need for change.

Black and silver

In the design office, I brought together all the Sony designers, who formerly worked in disparate product divisions. Everyone worked hand in hand to develop a unified, sophisticated identity that we would evoke in every Sony product. We worked on the copy and graphics for the product advertising even as we were refining the designs.

Simplicity is the essence of sophisticated design. In audio equipment and other consumer electronics products, basic black and silver or gray and silver furnished a minimalist color scheme that combined style and functionality gracefully. We achieved a striking effect by applying black enamel to die-cast aluminum bodies and then grinding off the paint lightly to expose a polished silver surface in selected patterns.

The TC-777 tape recorder

Morita had supervised the planning and design of Sony's first home tape recorder, the Model H, which debuted in 1951. Ten years later, I led the development of Japan's first all-transistor tape recorder, the TC-777. That product was an early exemplar of our new design strategy. It featured a then-unique gray-and-silver color scheme, which we carried over later into a high-end FM radio, the TFM-110. Another feature of the TFM-110, popularly known as the Eleven, was its nearly square profile. That was a fresh departure from the predominant oblong design for radios. The performance and bold styling of the TFM-110 proved extremely popular and helped inflate Sony's sagging market share in the radio sector.

In-house design competitions were effective in motivating our designers. We had about 40 designers in the early 1960s, and they vied enthusiastically for the chance to place their imprint on new products. In addition to the prestige of putting a design into the marketplace, each winner received a bottle of Johnny Walker Black Label scotch. Japan still imposed high tariffs on imported liquor, making Johnny Walker prohibitively expensive for routine consumption. Black Label was the epitome of luxury and a much-prized gift. Although I didn't drink, I made a point of picking up a couple of bottles for the design competitions whenever I traveled abroad. We'd display a bottle prominently in the design office when a competition was under way, and our designers spoke of "working for Johnny."

Fostering camaraderie was a high priority for me in managing the design office. A continuity of personnel prevailed in other divisions at Sony, but we had created the design office overnight by rounding up the company's designers. So I needed to devote special attention to nurturing a team spirit.

Sony traditionally took all its employees on a company trip each year. I took my team from the design office on a separate trip, however, and at a different time. Taking our trip separately reinforced our solidarity, and it gave us more opportunities to have fun. Recalling my excitement at debarking from Japan for Germany by ship, I proposed a brief voyage. Numerous Japanese were immigrating to South America at that time, and the ships that carried them called at the port of Yokohama en route from Kobe. Our design team took a train to Kobe and boarded ship for the cruise up the coast to Yokohama. Everyone had a great time, and the designers-only trip became an annual tradition.

Unified advertising

Measures for coordinating our advertising and product design work included moves to evoke a sophisticated and consistent corporate identity. We determined the most effective size and positioning for the Sony logo in newspaper advertisements of different sizes, and we established guidelines for ensuring adherence to that size and positioning in all our newspaper advertising.

Similarly, we conceived the advertising slogans in-house and mandated that they appear in a specified manner in all advertising during a specified period. We prepared templates for different kinds of advertisements and furnished them to all the editorial designers who worked on our advertising.

Sony had traditionally relied on advertising agencies for the creative content of its advertising. When I took over the advertising division, we began to produce our advertising internally. Our advertising agencies, however, charged the same amount for advertising placements, whether or not they produced the creative content. I demanded a discount commensurate with the creative work that we had shifted in-house, and that sparked a furor.

Japan's large advertising agencies earn most of their revenues through media brokerage. They charge hefty commissions on the space or time slots that they purchase for clients in print and broadcast media. Any creative work that they perform is commonly a throw-in included in the media commission. For the advertising agencies, the commission rates were sacrosanct. My call for discounts threatened to undermine their rigorously maintained wellspring of earnings.

The advertising agencies were unanimous in rejecting my demand out of hand. I was adamant, however, and threatened to withhold our advertising unless they complied. Sony's advertising budget was far smaller in the 1960s than it is today, but it had become large enough that my threat carried some weight, and the agencies finally came around.

I also ruffled feathers in the advertising industry with another reform. The advertising agencies refused to guarantee where in a newspaper an advertisement of any given size would appear. That ran counter to my notions of advertising strategy. Maximizing impact hinged on placing an ad in the optimal section of the newspaper—sports, TV listings, living, business, etc.—depending on the target audience and the size and orientation of the ad. I demanded the right to specify the page placement of our advertisements, and the agencies again resisted. My response was to place ads only when the agencies would guarantee where they would appear in the newspaper.

We broke from custom, too, in declining to use celebrities to pitch our products. I believed fervently in focusing attention on the products that our designers had worked so hard to shape and style. If the products lacked sufficient visual appeal to capture readers' attention, then something was wrong with our product design. Sony later cast celebrities in television advertising for commercials for television sets and video cameras, notwithstanding my initial resistance. The company's advertising in print media, however, continues to center to this day on product photos and explanations.

Automated control for tape recorders

User-friendly operation has always been even more important to the appeal of Sony products than styling or advertising. Making our tape recorders easy to use was a challenge that I undertook early on in my production division.

In those days, tape recorders obliged users to thread the tape between a capstan and a rubber pinch roller. That complexity was presumably part of the joy of ownership for hardcore audiophiles, but it was an unrelenting annoyance for most users. I conceived a mechanism that kept the pinch roller out of sight and out of mind until the tape was in place and the tape recorder was ready to play. We later developed a mechanism that threaded the tape recorder automatically. To simplify recording, we developed automatic level control. That eliminated the need for users to set the recording volume manually while keeping an eye on a sound level meter. Customers loved our advances in automating and otherwise simplifying tape recorder operation, and sales surged.

The Trinitron

Hosting the 1964 Summer Olympic Games was a postwar coming-out celebration for Japan as a reconstructed industrial democracy. The entire nation was alive with excitement in advance of the games. In that heady atmosphere, a team of Sony engineers was at work on an important new product technology: color television.

Sony was a latecomer to television manufacturing but had made waves in that product sector with some distinctive technologies. The company had famously deployed its transistor expertise, for example, in the world's smallest television. Launched in 1962, the microtelevision had a five-inch screen. It captured attention in the United States as a "tummy TV" because people could watch it while lying prone.

The lack of small, long-life batteries in those days impaired the portability that the tiny product could otherwise have afforded, and the success of the microtelevision in the marketplace was short lived. But the product occasioned something of a sensation in connection with an imperial visit. The Emperor and Empress honored Sony with a visit when the microtelevision was still in development, and Ibuka showed them a prototype. He cautioned them, however, that the technology was top secret and asked them not to mention it to anyone. A magazine reporter learned of that incident after the microtelevision went on the market, and the magazine ran a story under the headline, "Sony Muzzles Imperial Couple."

Ibuka was determined for Sony to secure a foothold in color televisions, but he wanted to gain that foothold with original technology. He hated the idea of simply following the pack into an established format. Sony would ultimately market a color television technology, Trinitron, that would showcase the company's knack for innovation and that would contribute greatly to sales and earnings. The story of the Trinitron, however, began inauspiciously.

U.S. manufacturers had been marketing color televisions since the 1950s, using the so-called shadow mask format for their picture tubes. A color picture tube had three cathode guns, one each for exciting the red, green, and blue phosphors on the screen. Tiny holes in the shadow mask let the electron beams from the three cathode guns reach the phosphors of the appropriate color, and the mask absorbed electrons that would otherwise reach phosphors of the wrong color.

The shadow mask color televisions on the market in the early 1960s were unsatisfactory in regard to color and brightness. Sony engineers, though, encountered a promising alternative at a trade show in New

York in 1961. The technology that caught their attention, called Chromatron, provided a brighter picture than anything the Sony engineers had ever seen. Sony secured the rights to the technology and began working on putting it into mass production.

The Chromatron was the brainchild of Nobel laureate Ernest O. Lawrence at the University of California at Berkeley. Developed originally for military applications, it used a single electron gun and an aperture grille of vertical wires in place of the shadow mask. The Chromatron could theoretically provide a picture six times brighter than the shadow mask format. That advantage and the uniqueness of the technology endeared Chromatron mightily to Ibuka. Sony unveiled a prototype Chromatron television in September 1964, the month that the Tokyo Olympics got under way. A few Chromatron televisions later appeared in stores, but they were fiendishly difficult and exorbitantly expensive to manufacture.

The engineers were counting on mass-production economies of scale to lower costs, but the mass-production technology itself proved troublesome. Ibuka finally bit the bullet and shifted Sony's color television development effort to what became the Trinitron. Launched in 1968, the Trinitron inherited some Chromatron technologies, notably, the aperture grille and the single electron gun. The Trinitron's gun, to be sure, fired three different beams for the red, green, and blue phosphors, whereas the Chromatron made do with a single beam. But the Trinitron delivered the prodigiously bright and clear picture that Ibuka had envisioned from the start, and it became phenomenally successful in televisions and, later, in computer monitors.

Technology's indispensable mate: product design

I had a third-person vantage on the launch of the Trinitron. Sony set up the joint venture CBS/Sony Records with CBS in 1968 to assert a presence in Japan's music marketplace, and I moved to the start-up company as a senior managing director. I became the president there in 1970 and, after the joint venture had attained strong growth momentum, returned to Sony in 1972 as a newly named managing director.

Sony's share of Japan's market for television sets surged initially on the strength of robust Trinitron sales, but it shrank as rival manufacturers countered the Trinitron's popularity with improvements in their shadow mask televisions. When I was repatriated to Sony, our market share in televisions was back down to about 10%—the same level where it had hovered before the launch of the Trinitron.

I led a sweeping redesign of our television sets to rekindle sales growth. Wood-grain patterns were the predominant finish for television cabinets at the time, but we adopted a finish that emphasized the plastic material. As for the channel changer, we replaced the dial with the still-unusual push-button format and mounted the buttons atop the 13-inch screen.

KV-1375 was the offical model name for the redesigned television, but our people nicknamed the product Citation—a moniker suggestive of the Triple Crown–winning racehorse memorialized by Cessna Aircraft Company in an eponymous line of business jets. The modernistic television went on sale in 1977 and was an immediate success, especially among young people. Our market share in color televisions surged to 14%.

A promotion to executive deputy president in 1976 removed me from direct responsibility for product planning, but I continued to keep a close eye on product-development activity at Sony. The next breakthrough television to emerge from that activity was the Profile Pro. Launched in 1980, that product was a modular affair that comprised a stand-alone monitor connected by cables to speakers, a control unit, and a selection of other equipment. The Profile Pro captured the imagination of the public, and several exhibitors at the 1980 Tokyo Motor Show used the new television in their booths to evoke leading-edge technology.

A concern with branding identity was evident even in the remote-control units for Sony television sets. We were steadfastly consistent, for example, in placing the channel buttons on the right and the vol-

The Sony television nicknamed Citation

ume buttons on the left. The era of multiple-television households had arrived, and consistency in control-panel layouts was a welcome convenience for consumers.

Pity the manager responsible for our television operations who had the temerity to try reversing the positions of the channel and volume buttons. He presumably believed he had a good reason for making the change. But as soon as I got wind of the impending change, I restored the buttons immediately to their proper places. We could ill afford to confuse consumers by revamping our design concepts every time our product-development managers changed.

A winning format for cassette tapes

Securing trademark rights and negotiating licensing arrangements with companies based outside Japan was my responsibility for several years. That facet of my work elicited an urgent call from Morita one day in my second year at the company. He had just flown back from Europe and was calling from the airport.

"Hey, I need you to go to Germany immediately. We might not be able to register the Sony name as a trademark there."

I soon learned that Agfa-Gevaert, the German manufacturer of photographic film, owned the trademark Soli in its camera operations. Agfa-Gevaert had filed a complaint that the names were so similar that ours infringed on their trademark. We persuaded the German authorities that our name was sufficiently different to justify a separate trademark. A bigger challenge arose later in Germany, however, in regard to our television technology for accommodating the Phase Alternating Line (PAL) format.

PAL is one of the three color-encoding systems used widely for television and video. The other two are the National Television Standards Committee (NTSC) and Séquentiel couleur à mémoire (SECAM) systems. PAL originated in Germany, NTSC in the United States, and SECAM in France. The German company Telefunken created the PAL format, but Sony developed original technology that allowed for handling PAL signals without relying on Telefunken's patented technology. Telefunken argued, nonetheless, that our technology infringed on their patents and tried to block our entry into the European television market.

Morita was adamant about the originality of our technology and assigned me the task of securing free access to the European market for Sony televisions. Our stance prevailed after a series of tough negotiations, and we managed to sell our televisions in Europe without paying any royalties to Telefunken.

Morita was always unyielding in the face of challenges to our rights. But Sony was a willing and conscientious partner as circumstances warranted. Witness our collaboration with the Dutch company Philips Electronics N.V. in establishing the dominant global standard for compact cassette tapes.

Philips and Germany's Grundig each approached Sony around the same time in the early 1960s about developing cassette tape formats jointly. Sony had launched a tape recorder in 1957 that employed reels encased in a "magazine." Our magazine-type tape recorder had not exactly taken the world by storm, however, and I recognized the need for a more-compelling format for encased tape products.

Approaching Sony on behalf of Philips was Wisse Dekker, then the head of Philips's far eastern operations and later to become the company's president. He invited me to visit Philips and met me in Munich to escort me personally in a private plane to the headquarters in Eindhoven. I had visited the headquarters with Ibuka when I was studying music in Germany, and our reception then had been less than ingratiating. This time, the people at Philips went out of their way to make me feel welcome. I marveled at the respect that Sony was beginning to command on the world stage.

Max Grundig, the president of the electronics manufacturer that bore his family name, made the case for his company. I had all the respect in the world for Grundig's technology. But Philips was far more global in the scope of its operations, and it held more patents in regard to cassette tape technology. I therefore declined Grundig's overtures and opted for a collaboration with Philips.

My decision earned the ire of Max Grundig. He argued angrily that Philips had merely imitated cassette tape technology developed earlier at his company. In fact, the U.S. company RCA had launched the world's first cassette tape product in 1958. RCA used tape a quarter-inch wide in units that it called "cartridges." The cartridges were bulky, however, and failed to take hold in the marketplace. For all I know, Grundig might well have been the first company to use the term "cassette tape."

Free cross-licensing

Philips's Dekker initially intended to charge Sony a licensing fee for the rights to the compact cassette tape technology. I insisted that Sony should have royalty-free access to the technology if our companies were to develop the format jointly. Dekker was eager to team with Sony, and he recognized the need for swift action in the race to establish a global standard. Some of his colleagues failed to see why Philips should share its patents with a then far smaller Japanese company. Dekker argued that Sony would be an increasingly valuable partner to Philips in the years ahead. He noted, especially, Sony's patents and technological strengths in the nascent market for video equipment.

Our companies ultimately arrived at a free cross-licensing arrangement. Each gained royalty-free access to its partner's patents in regard to magnetic storage in audio and video equipment. And Sony launched its first cassette tape recorder, the TC-100, in 1966.

The idea at Philips initially was to make its cassette tape technology available on a royalty-free basis only to Sony. Potential antitrust issues prompted Philips, however, to open the technology to all prospective manufacturers of cassette tape recorders. That occasioned swift and global growth in the market for cassette tapes and recorders. Even-bigger things were in store, meanwhile, for the Sony-Philips partnership.

The Compact Disc

Desktop computers, epitomized by Apple Computer's trailblazing models, proliferated in the 1970s. The digital revolution was under way, and it would change the course of consumer electronics profoundly. Sony introduced some products for digital tape recording, but we could see that disks were a more suitable medium for digital content.

Our engineers developed a system that allowed for recording up to 13 hours and 20 minutes of music on a disk. They demonstrated that system in 1977, but I had doubts about their approach. That much musical content would necessarily carry a hefty price tag—too hefty for the consumer market.

Just as we were mulling the commercial prospects for our digital technology, I received a message from L. F. Ottens, an old friend at Philips. Ottens was in charge of product development in Philips's audio equipment operations. He had worked closely with Dekker in developing the cassette tape format. Ottens said that he had something he wanted me to see and asked if I couldn't come to Eindhoven. Something about the message from Ottens suggested that I should go sooner rather than later. I visited the Philips headquarters in June 1978. Ottens greeted me and promptly produced an 11.5-centimeter optical disk from his pocket.

"This disk," he explained, "has the same 60-minute capacity as a cassette tape. We'd like Sony to work with us in establishing this as an industry standard."

Philips and Sony had achieved a historic success with the cassette tape format, and here was a chance to repeat that success with a new technology. Our resources were complementary and substantial. Philips was a leader in optical video disk technology, and it owned a large record company, PolyGram. Sony possessed world-class technology in digital processing, and we owned one-half of CBS/Sony.

I had long felt that moving beyond vinyl was essential to lasting growth for the record industry and had been an early proponent of optical disks. If we could agree on a technological format, Sony and Philips would be in an excellent position to transform the record industry. The devil is in the details, though, and coming to terms on the technological specifics proved daunting.

Philips's reasons for favoring an 11.5-centimeter disk had struck me as arbitrary. That size, argued Philips, would hold the same 60 minutes of music that a cassette tape could hold, was roughly equivalent to the diagonal dimension of the audio cassette tape, would fit in a suit-jacket pocket, would mesh well with car audio systems, and was consistent with Germany's Deutsche Industrienorm (DIN) industrial standards. It would not accommodate, however, a longish symphony, like Beethoven's *Ninth*.

We at Sony conducted a survey of classical music recordings and determined that a 12-centimeter disk capable of holding 75 minutes of music would accommodate 95% of the principal works. Our arguments proved persuasive, and Philips agreed to the 12-centimeter size—which did, incidentally, fit easily into the pocket on any suit jacket.

We also persuaded Philips to adopt 16-bit quantization rather than the 14-bit quantization it favored initially. The larger number of quantization bits entailed more-expensive technology, but it would ensure viability for the new format into the 21st century. Error correction was another subject of debate. Sony had developed highly advanced error-correction technology through its work on digital audio systems, and we fought successfully to incorporate a lot of that technology in the new system.

A valuable ally

A crucial ally in our development work on what became the Compact Disc was the great conductor Herbert von Karajan. I had maintained contact with him since Michiko Tanaka introduced us in 1956, when I was a student in Germany. We got together whenever concert engagements brought the conductor to Japan, and he took an active interest in our early work on digital recording equipment. Our engineers captured his attention by recording one of his rehearsals. He was startled at the quality of the sound and became a keen aficionado of Sony technology.

When I was visiting von Karajan's home in Salzburg one time, he led me into the basement. Arrayed before us were banks of Sony audio and video equipment. He had his performances recorded and edited on videotape, and he was a great adherent of Sony technology. Sony's fans included numerous famous personages, and we frequently

Von Karajan examining a prototype CD player

received requests from celebrities for discounts on our products. Never, though, did von Karajan make such a request.

Morita and I were grateful, of course, for von Karajan's patronage. We always demonstrated our latest products for him when he came to Japan, and he seemed to look forward to seeing and hearing what we were up to. The great conductor had a great rapport with Morita, especially, and enjoyed using the pool at Morita's home in Tokyo. Our close relationship with von Karajan deepened steadily as our work on digital audio technology progressed. When we revealed our plans for developing an optical-disk format, he announced instantly that he would participate in the project.

Von Karajan was clearly concerned with his legacy, and he was alert to any and all technological possibilities for preserving his performances faithfully. That included receptivity to technologies from manufacturers besides Sony. He experimented, for example, with a prototype digital tape recorder developed in the late 1970s by the U.S. manufacturer 3M Company.

Manufacturers of audio equipment established the Digital Audio Disk (DAD) Conference to work out a standard or standards for the impending audio-disk products. Sony was a member of the conference, but we soon saw that a consensus would not coalesce in time to keep up with the technological possibilities. So we went ahead and began developing a standard with Philips in 1979.

Sony and Philips concluded a joint-development contract, reached agreement on the broad outlines of a digital audio disk standard, and presented our standard to the DAD Conference as a fait accompli. We called our proposed standard the Compact Disc (CD) Digital Audio System.

Predictably, the Sony-Philips standard sparked a furor at the DAD Conference. Some of the members favored an electrostatic system developed by Victor Company of Japan. Others backed a mechanical system developed by Telefunken. The conference members ended up recognizing two standards in April 1981: our Compact Disc system and Victor's electrostatic system.

Von Karajan arranged for Sony and Philips to unveil a prototype CD system at the Salzburg Easter Festival in April 1981. Record company executives and music journalists from around the world assemble annually at that festival. The chance to demonstrate our CD system there was thus a golden opportunity to capture attention and generate publicity. Determined to make the most of that opportunity, we prepared our demonstration carefully.

A chief selling point for the Compact Disc was, as the name says, compactness. The equipment, however, was anything but compact.

That was before we had adopted highly integrated semiconductor devices for the circuitry, and we feared that the sight of the bulky setup would undermine the presentation. Our solution was to conceal the main equipment beneath a table and place only the disk mechanism atop the table. Leaving the power on for a prolonged period could cause the equipment to overheat and malfunction, so we also concealed an engineer under the table to turn on the power at the appropriate time.

Von Karajan appeared before the assembled guests at the presentation and held up a silver CD. He declared that our new technology delivered a sound exceedingly close to the original, far better than analog recording. Morita then related the story of the development of the CD format, and a Philips executive explained why his company and Sony had joined hands to develop the CD system. We all then fielded questions from members of the excited audience.

Heated opposition

How to respond to the CD format was a hot topic at the 1982 International Music Industry Conference, which convened near Athens. I attended the gathering with some engineers from our Tokyo headquarters and with Michael Schulhof, an executive from Sony Corporation of America who later became president of that subsidiary. We regarded the CD as a technology that would spur a new wave of growth for the record industry, and we naively expected the record companies to welcome the technology in that spirit. Instead, we encountered outright hostility.

One record executive didn't even wait for the end of Schulhof's presentation to stand up and denounce the CD format. He noted that the industry had a lot invested in the business of vinyl long-play (LP) records, and he questioned the need for a new format that would render that investment worthless. The executive also expressed misgivings about Sony and Philips pressing ahead unilaterally with a new standard. He and his colleagues acknowledged the superior sound quality of the CD technology, but they were disinclined to adopt a product format that they perceived as designed primarily to enrich Sony and Philips. Even executives from CBS, our joint venture partner in CBS/Sony, were cold and disdainful.

The frustrating experience in Greece revealed the futility of trying to win over the record industry in advance. We would need to go ahead and put our CD products into mass production and proselytize on the run. Our target for the product launch was October 1982, and I planned to announce the launch in August. More than the usual number of glitches arose, however, as the summer wore on.

Work on integrating the circuitry in semiconductor chips proceeded basically on schedule, but we fell behind in developing mass-production technology for the optical pickups. The pickups were unlike anything Sony or anyone had ever mass-produced. Achieving the required precision proved fiendishly difficult. Meanwhile, our record plant, which would produce the disks, was unable to achieve the required flatness with the polycarbonate substrate.

Uncertain about the prospects for the biggest product announcement of my career, I could have camped out at the office and pestered the engineers incessantly. Instead, I decided to put my faith in them and took a week off for summer vacation. Sure enough, they greeted me on my return with a series of gratifying reports. Yields were rising steadily on our production line for the optical pickups. And process improvements at the record plant had resolved the problems with the polycarbonate substrate.

We announced the product launch in Tokyo on August 31. The announcement was by Sony, Philips, PolyGram, and CBS/Sony. Newspapers and television networks jumped on the announcement eagerly and issued glowing reports of a "dream-come-true technology" and of "the dawn of the digital era." Opposition in the record industry remained fierce, however, and we knew that we had our work cut out for us in positioning the CD as a commercially viable alternative to vinyl.

Diminishing our joy at the launch announcement was the recent passing of Sony's president, Kazuo Iwama. He had led the building of Sony's semiconductor device operations, and the original technological capabilities of those operations had been indispensable to the CD development project. I took consolation in knowing that he had lived to see his semiconductor technology engender a crucially important new product.

IV

Ten Years to the Top in the Record Business

Morita called me into his office one October afternoon in 1967 and announced that he wanted to move into the music business, that he was considering a joint venture for that purpose with CBS, and that he wanted me to head the joint venture. A rival manufacturer, Victor Company of Japan, had secured a foothold in the record business. And Morita had long since concluded that a presence in the music business was a natural complement to our business in consumer electronics.

The Japanese government, meanwhile, had just relaxed its prohibition on foreign investment in the nation's music business, and foreign companies could henceforth own 50% of Japanese record companies through joint ventures with Japanese partners. Harvey Schein, then the president of CBS International and later to become the president of Sony Corporation of America, had come to Japan in search of a joint venture partner. Morita confided to me that he had just had lunch with Schein, who was building a global network of sales channels for CBS's records. Schein had apparently wearied of inconclusive negotiations with other Japanese companies and had turned his attention to Sony.

Morita had set up a lunch with Schein the day after receiving a call from CBS. The American, I would learn, had been impressed at Morita's decisiveness. Morita's prompt action contrasted sharply with the sluggish response characteristic of Japanese corporations.

I had become a member of Sony's board of directors in 1964 and was responsible for a vast range of work, including product development and design and advertising and public relations. A trusted and reliable right-hand man would be indispensable if I were to undertake a new challenge in the music business. Fortunately, the perfect candidate was available. Toshio Ozawa, had worked under me in the manufacturing division. He had displayed unparalleled skills in production management, and Sony had recently dispatched him to oversee the restructuring of an important supplier. That project was proceeding well, and the time had come to find a new place to exercise Ozawa's considerable capabilities.

Schein visited Sony headquarters a week after his lunch with Morita. He brought along Goddard Lieberson, the president of CBS's Columbia Group, and Walter Yetnikoff, a vice president at CBS International who was responsible for contracts. Morita, I, and other Sony executives soon reached an agreement with the visitors about the broad outlines of a joint venture. Schein and I would represent the two companies in working out the details.

Columbia and Columbia

A potential complication was a contract between Columbia and a Japanese namesake. Nippon Columbia supplied the vinyl records that CBS's Columbia Group sold in Japan. Established in 1910, Nippon Columbia had produced Japan's first record players and was the patriarch of the nation's record business. It acquired the Japanese rights to the Columbia name from the U.K. company Columbia Graphophone in 1931 and was the Columbia distributor in Japan before World War II. Nippon Columbia abandoned the foreign-sounding name for its products amid the xenophobia of the war years but resumed operating under that name after the hostilities ceased.

Columbia Phonograph, the original Columbia, cofounded CBS as Columbia Broadcasting System in 1927 but promptly severed ties with the broadcaster. CBS acquired its founder in 1938 and, after the war, sought unsuccessfully to regain the rights to the Columbia name in Japan. It settled instead for a series of licensing arrangements with Nippon Columbia, an increasingly tenuous compromise.

Management at the U.S. Columbia believed its artist portfolio and brand recognition warranted larger sales and market share in Japan. The U.S. executives chaffed at the lack of operating latitude imposed by their lack of a directly owned Japanese operation. They had tried to negotiate a joint venture agreement with Nippon Columbia, but their counterparts were unenthusiastic. Schein and his colleagues finally decided to find another partner. The fateful luncheon meeting between Schein and Morita all but sealed the deal with Sony.

Announcing the establishment of CBS/Sony Records

A complication that arose after we agreed to set up the joint venture was the matter of christening. We at Sony naturally argued for Sony-CBS as the better name for appealing to Japanese consumers. Our counterparts, however, were adamant about putting CBS first. We finally agreed on the name CBS/Sony Records on the basis of alphabetical order.

Building from the ground up

I worked on the preparations for the joint venture while heading three divisions at Sony. But after we established CBS/Sony Records in 1968, I moved to the new company as a full-time executive. Morita was nominally the head of CBS/Sony Records as its president, yet I was in charge of day-to-day operations as a senior managing director. CBS seconded none of its people to serve as full-time executives at the joint venture, leaving operational management entirely to Sony.

Our first challenge at CBS/Sony Records was to staff our company. Building a successful record company would mean creating a new and unique corporate culture. Sony had built a prominent and well-regarded identity in consumer electronics manufacturing but had no experience in the record business. I was determined to hire people who would bring fresh perspectives to our venture.

Managers at Japan's other record companies were doubly wary of our intentions. The launch of CBS/Sony Records signaled both the entry of a large foreign record company into their home market and a move by a consumer electronics company into their industry. Worried that we would pluck people from their companies, some of them appealed to the government to prohibit headhunting.

I recall asking Morita how in the world we would find enough people in time to go into business. He answered with characteristic aplomb, "Oh, something will work out." And it did.

We placed a large help-wanted ad in a national newspaper in March 1968. The ad announced, "We are looking for people to build CBS/Sony Records." It featured the new company's corporate logo, which incorporated the logos of both parent companies. The headline that preceded the body copy declared that "A new Sony venture is beginning," and we invited applications from "People who want to make musical dreams come true at CBS/Sony," "People who want to fulfill their potential at CBS/Sony," and "People who want to build CBS/Sony into the best record company in Japan."

Our ad listed 16 criteria for the kinds of people that we were seeking, and it assured readers that we welcomed applications from anyone "regardless of nationality, age, gender, academic attainment, or physical disability." We had written the ad ourselves, and we were proud of our work. The eye-catching ad was unlike anything that any Japanese company had ever placed in a Japanese newspaper.

I looked forward to the flood of applications that was certain to pour in. The initial response, however, was more a trickle than a flood. We received just six or so applications on the first day after the ad appeared and not many more over the next couple of days. I was despondent. I couldn't believe that our company and our recruiting pitch hadn't attracted more interest. Our administrative manager sulked off to the post office on the day after our postmark deadline to pick up any last-minute applications. He returned excitedly with two huge wicker baskets full of letters from prospective employees. In all, we received some 7,000 applications. We interviewed hundreds of people and ended up hiring about 80.

Breaking the mold

Only a handful of the people we hired had any experience in the record business. In my view, a stifling web of premodern commercial practices was retarding the growth and development of Japan's recording industry. I wanted to reform the industry, and I needed a team that was unbeholden to the industry's traditional practices.

Especially vexing was the vicious circle of indiscriminate distribution by the record companies and unconditional acceptance of unsold merchandise returned by record stores. The record companies foisted multifarious records—a lot of which were of dubious sales potential—on the record stores. In exchange for agreeing to stock those records, the stores were free to return any that didn't sell, no questions asked.

Record distribution in Japan was thus like pouring water through a sieve. It lacked the creative tension needed to focus the energies of distributors and vendors on identifying and offering records of compelling appeal. I vowed to the record stores that CBS/Sony Records would eschew hard-sell distribution, and I asked them to do their part by agreeing to return no more than 10% of our records that they stocked. In addition, I insisted on cash payment for the records that we distributed, instead of the customary six-month promissory notes.

Toshiba Corporation, another manufacturer of electronic equipment, had established a record venture—now Toshiba-EMI—before Sony and had also floated some proposals for modernizing Japan's record industry. The Toshiba proposals, though more modest than mine, had received severe criticism. My proposals sparked a veritable firestorm of vicious protest from the record stores and from their industry association.

Our salespeople fanned out across the nation to promote our records to retailers, but they encountered a generally hostile response from the store owners, who resented my efforts to reform the industry. Even our partners at CBS were disdainful of my approach. They feared that we would fail to get our products into the record bins in the marketplace and that the joint venture would be stillborn. I refused to compromise, however, confident that the industry would gradually recognize the wisdom of our approach.

Saved by Simon and Garfunkel

For our high-principled approach to business to have a chance of succeeding, we would need to offer convincing titles. A powerful title fell into our lap when CBS released Simon and Garfunkel's soundtrack album from the 1967 movie *The Graduate*. That movie was extremely popular in Japan, and its theme song, "The Sound of Silence," was a huge hit. Record store owners who had refused to even listen to our salespeople did an abrupt about-face and began placing orders. Some of them literally beat a path to our headquarters, packs on backs and cash in hand, to buy records. Each record store signed a purchasing contract as a condition for buying records, and we thus finally gained a nationwide network of sales outlets.

We also made important progress in signing prominent recording artists. Our early efforts in artist development centered on classical music, but we soon shifted our focus to popular music. Classical music accounted for about one-fourth of Japanese record sales and popular music for about three-fourths when Morita began mulling a move into the music business. But by the time we were up and running at CBS/Sony Records, popular music accounted for some 90% of record sales in Japan.

Pop music from the United States and the United Kingdom was much in demand among Japanese consumers, and CBS's portfolio of artists generated solid sales volume. Achieving the kind of sales growth that we envisioned, however, would depend on developing business in original recordings by Japanese artists.

Deciding how to proceed in cultivating Japanese pop music artists became the subject of heated debate at our company. In an early experiment, we signed the singer Carmen Maki. She had come to prominence in avant-garde stage productions by the enfant terrible of Japanese theater, Shuji Terayama, and was a truly gifted singer. Her rendering of "Sometimes I Feel Like a Motherless Child" captured the hearts of Japanese listeners and rewarded our faith in Carmen with hefty sales. It was a big hit of 1969 and earned Maki and us a spot in a much-watched musical-variety special aired annually on New Year's Eve by Japan's public television broadcaster, NHK.

Masatoshi Sakai, a CBS/Sony employee who formerly worked at Nippon Columbia, helped steer our artist strategy in a fortuitous direction. He argued that the future of Japanese pop music lay in cute young singers to be marketed as prepackaged "idols." Sakai was persuasive, and his judgment proved prescient. Musical ability was secondary to "cuteness" as a consideration in finding and nurturing potential idols, male and female.

CBS/Sony Records had more than its share of success in the idol business, and our biggest success of all was the inimitable Momoe Yamaguchi. A star of iconic stature, Yamaguchi accompanied idol-like good looks with genuine musical talent and a knack for acting, which she exhibited in several successful films. She was Japan's best-loved idol of the 1970s and retired at her peak after a momentous farewell concert in 1980.

We were more aggressive than our better-established rivals out of necessity: as a new company, we had no stable of artists to draw on and needed to build a pool of talent from scratch. Sakai saw Yamaguchi on the television talent show *A Star Is Born* and worked assiduously to recruit her, while she was still in junior high school, for CBS/Sony Records. When he brought her in for an interview, I recognized a presence that would capture the heart of a nation and decided immediately to sign her to a contract. Yamaguchi more than justified my confidence as she mastered her craft and grew steadily as an artist. Her recordings remain as fresh today as when they were just released. She was a master of nuance and imparted unsuspected subtlety to lyrics in bringing songs to life.

Although CBS/Sony Records and other record companies took part in identifying and cultivating singers, we entrusted the work of managing their careers to talent agencies. We worked closely with those agencies in forecasting trends in demand and in analyzing the different judges' proclivities in important musical awards. Together, we devised musical and promotional strategies aimed at optimizing the performance of our artists and at maximizing our record sales.

I have been disappointed at the aesthetic direction of Japanese pop music since the 1980s, but that is presumably more a critique of my aging taste than of the ever-evolving world of pop music. Each generation demands a new set of musical criteria, and I am long past the age where I could possibly function as a judge of commercial potential in the music marketplace. Still, the monosyllabic crassness of contemporary pop lyrics makes me all the more nostalgic for Momoe Yamaguchi's elegantly nuanced phrasing.

Aiming for No. 1 in record sales

I set four goals for CBS/Sony Records when we established the company in 1968. One, become Japan's leader in record sales within 10 years. Two, erect our own headquarters building as soon as possible. Three, pay the highest salaries in the Japanese record industry. And four, build our own factory for pressing records. Achieving those goals became a personal quest, and we marked steady progress. I received the title of president of CBS/Sony Records in April 1970 and retained that position after becoming a managing director at Sony in June 1972. CBS/Sony Records achieved all four of my goals and, for the most part, within my 10-year time frame.

The joint venture became Japan's biggest record company in sales in 1979. That was 11 years after its establishment and, strictly speaking, a year late, but it was a gratifying fulfillment of a bold target. We were well on the way toward fulfilling my goals as early as August 1973. That was when we held a two-day gala at a Tokyo hotel to celebrate the fifth anniversary of CBS/Sony—we had dropped "Records" from the name that month.

We had fulfilled the goal of occupying our own headquarters building even as we were making preparations for our fifth-anniversary gala. Morita and I had tremendous admiration for William Paley, an heir to a cigar fortune who purchased CBS in 1928 and built it into a broadcasting giant, and for Frank Stanton, who served as CBS president from 1946 to 1971. Both men were visionaries, and both were superb managers.

Stanton was a great believer in the importance of corporate style, and he had micromanaged the construction and furnishing of the CBS Building. That 38-story structure, designed by the great architect Eero Saarinen and opened in 1965, stands in midtown Manhattan at the corner of 52nd Street and Sixth Avenue. A supremely elegant work of architecture, it features dark granite cladding, which has earned the building and its owner the nickname Black Rock.

We built the CBS/Sony headquarters building beside the Kanda River—the outer moat of the Imperial Palace—in Tokyo's Ichigaya district. Morita and I were determined to create a headquarters suggestive of the elegance of the CBS Building, and I supervised the architects closely through every stage of the project.

I took an interest in unseen elements of the building, such as the plumbing, as well as in the architectural aesthetics. The water pipes are usually the first thing in a building to go bad and to require extensive maintenance work. I insisted on testing different kinds of pipe, including stainless steel. The results confirmed my suspicion that stainless steel would provide longer-life durability. Our new headquarters became the first building in Japan to contain extensive plumbing of stainless steel. I was similarly demanding in regard to the elevators and the air conditioning.

Cost was another subject of my scrutiny. Thanks to fastidious cost management, our headquarters cost only one-tenth as much to build per square foot as the CBS Building. I even worked to minimize the cost of moving. We gave each employee one cardboard box for packing personal effects. Anything more than would fit in the box they could take home or leave behind. We had bought new furniture for the new headquarters, meanwhile, and the proceeds from selling our old furniture to Sony affiliates basically covered the bill from the movers.

Getting the corporate culture right

Corporate culture is all but impossible to change once it takes shape, so I wanted to generate the right kind of atmosphere from the start. The music industry is a famously freewheeling business, and the atmosphere at CBS/Sony was highly relaxed. We were demanding of retailers in insisting that they curtail the amount of returned merchandise and in demanding from them payment in cash. So we needed to set a good example in regard to basic behavior.

Punctuality was a special emphasis. People in the music business are notoriously lax about time. We gave quartz watches, a new and novel technology at the time, to all our employees. And we decreed that we would not admit anyone to meetings more than one minute past the scheduled starting time. The world is rife with uncertainty, of course, and tardiness is sometimes unavoidable. But an organization will fall hopelessly behind if its members get the idea that being five minutes late is acceptable.

Expenses require equally rigorous monitoring. I passed my eyes over all the expense reports submitted by our employees. And I sent the reports back to the employees' superiors whenever I noted anything amiss.

Ozawa succeeded me as president of CBS/Sony in 1990 and performed admirably in maintaining the company's momentum. Sony acquired CBS Records in 1988, and CBS/Sony changed its name to Sony Music Entertainment in 1991.

V

Semiconductors

Recognizing the potential of the transistor gave Sony a head start in consumer electronics, and creatively tapping the potential of semiconductor devices has contributed immensely to the company's growth ever since. Kazuo Iwama, my predecessor as president at Sony, justly receives credit for establishing a solid foothold for Sony in semiconductors.

Iwama, a year older than Morita, grew up next door to the Sony cofounder in Nagoya. Morita, as the eldest son in his family, would ordinarily have inherited his family's sake-brewing business, but he entrusted the business to a younger brother to join Ibuka in establishing Sony (then Tokyo Tsushin Kogyo). Iwama, on the other hand, was the youngest of four sons in a family of eight siblings. He majored in geophysics at the University of Tokyo and worked as a researcher at a seismic laboratory after graduating. Ibuka and Morita were enthralled of Iwama's technological expertise, and they invited him to join their new venture. He accepted and came aboard in September 1946—a month after wedding Morita's younger sister Kikuko.

Ibuka was a technological genius, and Morita could hold his own in even the most sophisticated technological debates. Iwama excelled both of Sony's founders, however, in probing theoretical analysis. His technological acumen shone in the reports he filed from the United States while inspecting Western Electric semiconductor plants. William Shockley, John Bardeen, and Walter Brattain had invented the transistor in 1948 at AT&T Bell Labs, and Western Electric, another AT&D subsidiary, held crucial patents for the transistor.

Transistor technology had caught Ibuka's attention during a fact-finding trip to the United States, and he had quickly foreseen that semiconductor devices would replace vacuum tubes in electronic equipment. No one—not even Western Electric—was producing transistors yet in large volumes, and Ibuka was determined for Sony to be a pioneer in the nascent product sector. He initiated contact with AT&T to secure the rights to the technology. The upshot was an expensive licensing contract with Western Electric.

So we secured the right to develop transistors—and at a hefty cost—but we had no idea how to put them into mass production. Western Electric was little help initially. Our licensing contract pertained only to the basic technology and did not cover production processes. Ibuka and Morita pleaded with Western Electric to provide some useful insight into transistor manufacturing. The American company finally relented and allowed us to have a look at its plants.

Choosing the best person to visit the Western Electric plants became a matter of vigorous debate. Technological expertise and English competence were compelling prerequisites. Iwama emerged as the consensus candidate. His technological expertise was unquestioned—Ibuka had named him to head our newly established semiconductor division—and he was conversant in English as an avid reader of technical magazines from overseas.

Iwama traveled to the United States in February 1954 and became a fixture at Western Electric's semiconductor plants for two months. His hosts would not provide him with any technical specifications about their manufacturing equipment, but they gave him generally free run of the premises. Iwama prepared numerous dense reports of several pages each and mailed them to his colleagues at Sony during his sojourn.

The Iwama Reports, as they became known, were indispensable stepping-stones for Sony's engineers in developing manufacturing processes for semiconductor devices. Before long, Sony-branded transistor radios were pouring out of our plants and into the world marketplace. Thus did Sony become an indisputably global brand.

The next step

A subsequent breakthrough in semiconductors that also contributed definitively to strengthening Sony's global presence was the charge-coupled device (CCD). The CCD, invented by Willard Boyle and

George Smith at AT&T Bell Labs in 1970, was a quantum leap in converting visual images into electrical signals. More compact, more affordable, and more efficient than earlier devices for image-to-signal conversion, the CCD essentially spawned the consumer market for video cameras, and it remains the core component in digital video and still cameras.

Iwama worked at Sony's U.S. operations from 1971 to 1973 and was an early proponent of CCDs as a paradigm-busting technology. He gained the opportunity to translate his conviction into action on returning to Japan. Iwama became a deputy president at Sony and the director of the company's research center, and he promptly declared his intention to position Sony as a central player in CCDs.

I had returned to Sony headquarters from CBS/Sony the year before Iwama's repatriation to Japan. He spoke to me often and enthusiastically of the exciting prospects for CCDs. Those prospects were less than convincing, however, to the casual observer. In a CCD image of a human hand, you could just barely make out five fingers.

Iwama at Sony's research center

My interest in the CCDs under development at Sony was more than casual. Although I continued to serve as president of CBS/Sony, I resumed my former duties in overseeing product planning and design, and I assumed new responsibilities in supervising overall corporate planning. Those latter responsibilities included monitoring the budgeting for the CCD development effort.

"Ohga-san, we're going to need a lot of money again this year," Iwama would say with a sly grin whenever we met. "And we're not even going to recover your investment by the end of the century. Sorry about that."

Developing commercially viable CCDs was indeed a stupendously difficult task. Fortunately, Sony's corporate culture was amenable to expenditures of almost any size when people really believed in the cause. "I'm keeping my fingers crossed," was my standard reply to Iwama. And I did my part to secure the funding that he needed.

Sony was still not mass producing CCDs when Iwama succeeded Morita as the president of Sony in 1976. Even when we unveiled the world's first CCD-based color video camera in 1980, we were still far from mass production. Our CCD video cameras were the first video cameras that airlines installed on aircraft to monitor takeoffs and landings. Yields were extremely low in our CCD production processes, however, and the prices for our CCD video cameras were unavoidably exorbitant.

Iwama was impatient to raise yields and lower prices to position the CCD as a truly mass-production technology applicable to mass-consumption products. Sadly, his passing in 1982 prevented him from seeing that dream fulfilled. Responsibility for completing Iwama's quest passed to me as his successor, and I maintained our vigorous commitment to the CCD development program.

We finally succeeded in putting in place a platform for mass producing CCDs in 1983 at our Kagoshima Plant, in Kyushu. Eager to share our accomplishment with Iwama, the members of the development team and I visited his grave. We took along the first mass-produced CCD and affixed it to the back of the gravestone.

The fallout from defeat in the desktop calculator wars

Iwama's obsession with CCDs stemmed partly from Sony's ignominious performance years earlier in desktop calculators. Our company had staked out an early position in calculators, but we had ended up withdrawing from that market under pressure from the volume-oriented tactics of our chief competitors. For Iwama, the CCD development effort was a means of remotivating the demoralized engineers in our semiconductor operations.

Sony's semiconductor operations had worked wonders in creating transistors for our successful lines of radios, television sets, and videotape recorders. The facilities at the Atsugi Plant, our flagship semiconductor plant just outside Tokyo, were the company's crown jewels.

Our Atsugi Plant produced mountains of transistors every month, and amid those mountains was a large hill of transistors that had fallen just short of our specification standards. A plant engineer hated the idea of discarding those transistors, which were not essentially defective. He came up with the idea of using them in desktop calculators, where they would more than satisfy the required specifications.

Expectations were high when the Atsugi Plant unveiled the world's first electronic desktop calculator for homes. That was in spring 1964, just a few months before the Tokyo Olympics were to open. We called our inaugural calculator the MD-5, but the name became Sobax when we began mass producing an improved model in 1967. The name was to suggest Sony electronic abacus.

Casio and Sharp were already mass marketing desktop calculators and were devoting high priority to those products in R&D and in manufacturing and marketing. They presented us with a stark choice: make a large commitment to calculators or exit the market.

Calculators occupied a position on the periphery of the computer sector. Sony management had approved the development of the Sobax in the name of augmenting our product portfolio in consumer electronics. We could see, however, that establishing a competitive position in calculators would oblige us to develop a new set of capabilities in computer technology.

Ibuka felt that Sony had no business competing with the likes of IBM, and he had resolved to steer clear of the computer sector. Just about everyone concerned, notwithstanding the understandable disappointment at Atsugi, agreed with the decision to discontinue the Sobax.

Sony, of course, would later return triumphantly to the computing sector with the Vaio line of laptop computers and with the PlayStation game consoles. And the foundation that Iwama laid in developing and manufacturing semiconductor devices would remain a core strength for the company.

The scientific and technological creativity of the R&D team that Iwama built was amply evident in Sony's continuing stream of successful products. That creativity was also evident in the 1973 Nobel Prize in Physics that Leona Esaki received for research conducted at Sony. Esaki shared the physics prize with the Norwegian Ivar Giaever and the Briton Brian Josephson for discovering electron tunneling. He also gained fame for the Esaki diode, a device that employs the electron-tunneling phenomenon. Esaki's achievement of historic breakthroughs in a corporate R&D center is a tribute to the freedom he enjoyed under Iwama.

Note, too, that the transistors and CCDs developed by Iwama's team contributed to Sony's performance directly as stand-alone products, as well as through their applications in Sony products. We earned large sums by selling semiconductor devices and licensing pertinent patent rights to other manufacturers. Even the technical standards for the Compact Disc (CD) Digital Audio System that Sony developed with Philips owed a great deal to work by Iwama's engineers.

Meanwhile, Iwama's teasing insistence that we would never recover our CCD investment by the turn of the century proved overly pessimistic. Income from the CCDs had basically covered the cost of their development by the end of the 1990s. That is testimony to Iwama's foresight in recognizing commercial potential and to his brilliance in managing the required development effort.

Ibuka and Morita achieved celebrity status through their charismatic and iconoclastic management style and, of course, through Sony's prodigious growth under their leadership. Iwama is a less-familiar figure to the general public, partly because his untimely death abbreviated his term as president. He was a seminal force in building the company, however, and he ranks alongside Ibuka and Morita in the Sony pantheon.

VI

At the Helm

Our official corporate funeral for Iwama in August 1982 was the first for Sony. I selected a recording of Fauré's *Requiem* to play during the ceremony. The recording was one that I had made for the purpose of having played someday at my own funeral, but I dedicated it to Iwama. Numerous personages from the public and private sectors attended the funeral in an outpouring of respect for the departed.

After the sad farewell, Sony's board of directors convened to choose Iwama's successor. Morita collared me in the hallway on the way to the meeting and confirmed that he would nominate me as Sony's fifth president. Iwama had succeeded Morita, who had succeeded Ibuka. Tamon Maeda, Ibuka's father-in-law and a former government minister, had served as the company's inaugural president.

Morita's nomination was hardly a surprise. Ever since Sony had repatriated me from CBS/Sony, he had referred repeatedly to "when

At the press conference to announce the naming of the author to the presidency of Sony

you become president." And I had served as Sony's de facto acting president during the last year of Iwama's illness. So I had expected to take the helm one day, but I never expected that day to come so soon.

Seated beside Morita at a press conference after the meeting, I expressed my determination as president to "maximize the brand value of the four letters of the Sony name." The mass media were predictably bemused at the selection of a former musician to head a prominent corporation. But I could hardly afford to allow the less-than-gratifying reception from the media to distract me from the work at hand. We were preparing to launch our first CD products, and I needed to concentrate on fulfilling Iwama's digital vision.

Eleven manufacturers of audio equipment announced plans to launch CD players based on our format. The response from consumers, however, was generally lukewarm. Part of the reason for the unenthusiastic market reception was unfamiliarity with the technology. Even at CBS/Sony, employees wondered aloud how we could obtain sound from disks that had no grooves.

A bigger stumbling block was the high price of the CD players. The manufacturer's suggested retail price in Japan for the first Sony CD player, the CDP-101, was ¥168,000. That was equivalent to more than $650 at that time and was more than most consumers were prepared to pay for a "record player."

CBS/Sony was an invaluable source of content offerings in the new format, beginning with Billy Joel's *52nd Street*. Not until CD player prices dropped below ¥50,000, however, did sales really begin to take off. In autumn 1984, Morita issued the order to offer our new D-50 CD player at that price level. He was determined to build sales momentum, even if that meant selling the product at a loss. His judgment, once again, proved right on the mark. Sales of CD players and music CDs surged. By 1986, more titles were available on CDs than on LP records.

A Sony CD factory

In-house capabilities for manufacturing records had contributed to the success of CBS/Sony, and manufacturing capabilities for CDs helped us kick-start the market for the CD format. The first CD players and CDs went on sale in October 1982. That was just two months after we had brought the product and production technology to the levels deemed suitable for marketing. Enabling us to ramp up our production that quickly was the optical-disk manufacturing technology developed at our Shizuoka Plant.

The changing of the guard in recorded music

Our initial CD offerings numbered 50 albums. The Shizuoka Plant enabled us to produce a growing portfolio of music CDs despite fierce opposition from the record industry. It also helped us promote the new format by manufacturing CDs for other vendors of recorded music. Later, the plant produced PlayStation CDs and DVDs and movie DVDs, too.

Timing is of the essence in the music business. Music vendors need to be able to crank up production at the drop of a hat when titles show promise. CBS had relied on Nippon Columbia for the vinyl records it sold in Japan, and our joint venture counterparts there insisted that CBS/Sony should do likewise and thereby avoid incurring the expense of building a record plant. They failed to gauge the antipathy that they had aroused at Nippon Columbia by casting their lot with Sony. Nippon Columbia, having lost the marketing rights to Columbia titles, was not about to settle for simply supplying the vinyl records.

I saw that we would need an in-house manufacturing operation that would produce the records that we needed, when we needed them, and in the volumes that we needed. Reliably high quality was another factor in my reasoning. Records were still something of a luxury item in Japan. Consumers regarded their record purchases as investments, and they were fastidious in caring for the records. Customers were extremely demanding in regard to product quality, so we would need to fulfill exacting standards in our record manufacturing.

Our partners at CBS finally relented and agreed to the construction of a record plant. The next issue was location. Somewhere between Tokyo and Osaka made sense in regard to distribution logistics. We selected a site on a broad expanse of flat land near the sea in a Shizuoka Prefecture town called Oigawa. Morita had called my attention to the area around the time that we established CBS/Sony Records. He had observed the landscape from the company plane on a flight back to Tokyo from Osaka and had thought it might make a good site for a factory someday.

Recalling Morita's suggestion, I called the mayor of Oigawa, who offered to show me around personally. In rubber boots, we strolled between rice fields and surveyed prospective plant sites. The mayor was alert to the importance of pure water in manufacturing records, and he explained that a virtual river passed under the ground on which we were standing. Subsequent survey work verified his assertion. Good water would thus be readily available, and the logistics, too, were promising. Japan's first Shinkansen bullet train passed nearby, and we discovered that a planned freeway would also pass through the vicinity. Morita was delighted to hear that our surveys had borne out his airborne hunch.

The Shizuoka Plant, completed in autumn 1968, helped establish the Sony tradition of accompanying electronic products with complementary media. Refining the manufacturing technology for LP records took time, however, and we initially continued to outsource the pressing of classical music LPs, the most technologically demanding records.

Producing the classical LPs for us was the Victor Company of Japan. That was at a time when Japan's other record companies wanted nothing to do with CBS/Sony Records, and I will always be grateful to Hitoshi Momose, then the president of the Victor Company of Japan, for his openhearted generosity. Momose's company was a Sony rival in consumer electronics, but Morita had gone out of his way to maintain good relations. Morita informed Momose promptly, for example, of the plan at Sony to establish a joint venture with CBS, and Momose remained a trusted confidant.

Sony aloft

Morita's bird's-eye discovery of the site for the Shizuoka Plant was a fringe benefit of Sony's early acquisition of a company aircraft. Our first plane was a single-engine, propeller-powered Beechcraft. Morita loved that plane and took every opportunity to fly in it, mainly on round-trips between Tokyo and Osaka. Corporate planes have long been common in the United States, where the vast distances make an issue of executive mobility. Air access is less essential in compact Japan, and Sony was, to my knowledge, the first Japanese company to acquire a corporate plane. Our executives made the decision to purchase a plane in 1962, my third year as a full-time employee.

I had always loved trains and other contrivances that moved, and I began stopping by the Tokyo aircraft operations of the big trading company C. Itoh (now Itochu). That company supplied Japanese airlines with propeller aircraft manufactured by Beech Aircraft for training airliner pilots. I became acquainted with the technical manager of C. Itoh's aircraft operations, and he suggested buying a corporate plane for Sony. Morita was highly amenable to the idea when I broached the subject, but Sony's chairman, Michiharu Tajima, angrily rejected the very idea of a corporate plane as an extravagant luxury.

Tajima was a former schoolmate of Maeda, the president. He had an impeccable pedigree in finance, both in the private sector and in government, and he later served as an official in the Imperial Household Agency. The cost of a propeller plane was entirely manageable in the context of Sony's large and growing sales volume. But Tajima's objection was understandable, and I was startled at Morita's determined counterargument.

"We are entering an era when owning an executive plane will be the mark of a first-rate corporation," insisted Morita. "If you can't see that, you don't deserve to be called the chairman of this company."

The ferocity of Morita's rebuttal caught Tajima off guard. "Well, if you feel that strongly about it," he said, "then do as you please."

My acquaintance at C. Itoh introduced a former navy pilot to fly our new plane. But I soon got the itch to take the controls and began studying clandestinely. I earned pilot's licenses in 1972 for our single-engine Beechcraft and in 1974 for twin-engine propeller aircraft and for the Cessna Citation jet.

My passengers over the years included Ibuka, Morita, and numerous other Sony executives and employees. The flying was uniformly uneventful, with a notable exception one time over the island of Hawaii. I was carrying Ibuka, and we were to land at Kona International Airport. We arrived after the airport's 9 p.m. closing time, however, and the lights were out on the control tower and on the runway.

Ibuka had nerves of steel, but even he was visibly concerned. I checked the Jeppesen navigation manual and learned that clicking the communication frequency of the control tower four times would turn on the runway lights. Hoping against hope that things would actually work as advertised, I took the plane up and around for another pass and clicked the control tower frequency: once, twice, three times, four times. Sure enough! The runway lit up like Times Square, and we coasted in for a safe landing.

My only really life-threatening aviation experience was the crash of a helicopter in which I was riding as a passenger. That occurred in 1979 when, as a Sony executive deputy president, I flew across Tokyo Bay to visit our Kisarazu Plant, in Chiba Prefecture. We were just four meters above the ground on our descent when a freak gust tossed the helicopter upward and then slammed it into the ground.

Miraculously, the pilot and passengers escaped with injuries no more serious than the contusions and strains incurred in exiting hurriedly through the front of the burning hulk. The pilot neglected to turn off the engine, however, and the still-turning rotor tragically took the life of one of the plant employees who had raced forward to help.

An ambulance took all of the helicopter occupants to a local hospital for examinations. X-rays revealed no fractures in any of my bones, but the physicians urged a precautionary period of rest. Morita would have none of that, however, and dispatched a helicopter to bring me back to Tokyo. I protested that I never wanted to even see a helicopter again, much less ride in one of the confounded contraptions. Morita was adamant, however, and I followed his orders.

Persistent pain in my back drove me to undergo an examination at a Tokyo hospital. There, the physicians discovered a fracture in my spine and prescribed three months of rest away from work. No sooner had I begun to comply with the physicians' instructions than Morita intervened once again. He dispatched me to the United States for talks with CBS. Still bound and looking more mummy than businessman, I headed across the Pacific in a reclining seat on a jumbo jet.

An illustrious copilot

A shared love of piloting jet planes, even more than a shared interest in audio equipment, underlay my friendship with the great conductor Herbert von Karajan. The maestro came to Japan in autumn 1973 to conduct a commemorative concert in the newly completed NHK

Hall. I was tied up with work and, anyway, had not received a personal invitation, so I was at the office on the night of the concert. A call came from von Karajan's personal assistant, demanding to know why I was not at the concert. She reported that he had something important to discuss with me and wanted me to come immediately to NHK Hall.

As soon as I made way into von Karajan's dressing room, he happily produced a large sheet of paper. I momentarily assumed it to be a musical score but promptly discovered something decidedly different: a detailed diagram of an aircraft cockpit.

"This," announced von Karajan proudly, "is the cockpit in the plane that I am going to buy. What do you think?"

I could see immediately that the aircraft he was preparing to purchase was one of the sort flown by casual amateurs, and I told him so.

"Maestro, this is not the plane for you."

"But I've already ordered it."

In the cockpit

He insisted that I come to his suite at the Hotel Okura the next morning to continue the discussion. I did as he requested and explained my objections to his intended purchase. A better choice for him, I suggested, was the Dassault Falcon jet, one of which we had recently purchased at Sony.

About a year and a half later, I stopped in at a Falcon training center outside New York City for a scheduled lesson. Punctuality is the rule in scheduling time on flight simulators, so I was a bit peeved to hear that the preceding lesson was running overtime and that I would need to wait. My displeasure turned to delight, however, when the person who emerged from the simulator turned out to be von Karajan.

"Mr. Ohga, you were right. I sold the other plane and bought a Falcon. And whenever I buy a plane again, I will talk with you first."

Von Karajan thereupon began addressing me in letters and faxes as "my copilot." But when I became the president of Sony in 1982, he informed me in a congratulatory message that he would thereafter address me as "captain."

A 13-hour shareholders' meeting

The "captain" salutation from von Karajan notwithstanding, my work changed little on becoming Sony's president. I basically continued performing the duties I had been handling for the past year on behalf of the ailing Iwama, so I was slow in gaining a visceral sense of having taken the helm. A gut-level awareness of my new responsibilities finally arrived with a bang in January 1984. It arrived in the form of our annual shareholders' meeting—my second as president.

A lamentable fixture in Japan's stock market until recent years was a kind of extortion at the hands of so-called *sokaiya*—literally, "shareholders' meeting attenders." The *sokaiya*, essentially a category of organized criminals, exploited the Japanese preoccupation with decorum. Institutional shareholders—insurance companies and banks—owned most of the shares of publicly listed corporations in Japan. They rarely sold their shareholdings, and the annual meetings were little more than ceremonies for formalizing decisions vetted in advance with the principal shareholders. Not until several years later would any semblance of U.S.-style shareholder activism arise in Japan.

Short and uneventful shareholders' meetings were a point of pride for corporate managements. *Sokaiya* made their living by acquiring small shareholdings—just enough to entitle them to attend the annual shareholders' meetings—and by threatening to disrupt the meetings with embarrassing questions and motions unless the companies bought their silence. Companies that refused to pay faced the prospect of marathon shareholders' meetings. The assembled *sokaiya* would harangue the companies' executives with all manner of abuse and, sometimes, with genuinely troubling revelations. Underlying their cash demands was the implicit threat of physical violence, and they occasionally fulfilled that threat, sometimes fatally.

A law enacted in 1983 outlawed corporate payments to *sokaiya*, and the subsequent enforcement of that law has since largely eliminated the scourge. I had always despised the practice of paying tribute and was more than happy to ensure that Sony cease all such payments. The *sokaiya*, their survival at stake, were determined to assert a still-threatening presence, irrespective of the new law. Sony, as an increasingly prominent Japanese corporation, made an ideal target.

Sokaiya from throughout Japan converged on our 1984 shareholders' meeting. They began by submitting a series of mischievous motions, which delayed the start of the meeting more than 30 minutes. Crass rowdiness was the stock-in-trade of the *sokaiya*, and as the chair of the meeting I needed to call repeatedly for order.

The questions raised by the *sokaiya* centered on Sony's deteriorating position in the competition between our Betamax video format and the VHS format championed by our rival Matsushita Electric Industrial (Panasonic). They came as a continuing barrage of abuse, much of it directed at me personally. We fielded the questions patiently and dealt with the motions in accordance with the meeting rules but ceded nothing to extortion.

Our meeting convened at 10 a.m. and continued through the afternoon and into the night. The *sokaiya* eventually tired of the exercise and began dispersing as the night wore on, and the meeting ended around 11:30 p.m. I had thought that Sony would win applause for facing down the *sokaiya*, but the first questions from reporters after the meeting exposed the naivety of that expectation.

The reporters wanted to know what we had done wrong to have occasioned such a trying shareholders' meeting. True to the tone of their questions, the newspaper coverage the next day was generally negative in regard to Sony. As I recall, the *Mainichi Shimbun* was alone among the leading daily newspapers in acknowledging the propriety of our approach.

The acquisition of CBS Records

Even while facing down the *sokaiya*, I faced a demand from CBS for an increased dividend payout by CBS/Sony. The joint venture had consistently paid annual dividends to its parents equivalent to 100% of the company's paid-in capital. CBS called for doubling the dividend to an amount equivalent to 200% of the joint venture's paid-in capital. That would have meant drawing on retained earnings accumulated through the blood, sweat, and tears of the employees at CBS/Sony. It was a demand that I could not possibly accept.

William Paley and Frank Stanton, two giants who had steered CBS to greatness, had withdrawn from day-to-day management. At the helm was Lawrence Tisch. His surname meant "desk" in German, and Tisch was every bit the desktop calculator. He calculated that Sony's success in CDs ought to position our joint venture with CBS to double its dividend payout.

CBS and Sony had launched CBS/Sony Records as a 50:50 joint venture capitalized at ¥720 million. I proposed that the parents facilitate CBS's demanded increase in the dividend payout by doubling their investments in the venture. That mollified Tisch for the time being, but CBS soon began to clamor for more of the joint venture's retained earnings.

The exchange value of the yen had spiked in the wake of the Plaza Accord of 1985, and Japanese companies had embarked on a veritable feeding frenzy of investment in U.S. hotels, golf courses, and other properties. Tisch seemed to feel that CBS/Sony was wasting opportunities by letting its financial liquidity rest in Japan. I had no interest whatsoever in hotels or golf courses, but I acceded to the wishes of our joint venture partners and inspected a series of prospective investments, including a hotel in Hawaii. We ended up purchasing a large lemon grove in California, though I never overcame my doubts about the pertinence of the investment to our business.

In another move to assuage Tisch, we proposed that CBS/Sony build a U.S. record plant for CBS Records. Tisch was delighted with the idea and suggested that CBS/Sony then sell the mooted U.S. plant to Sony and remit the proceeds to CBS. That response was a telltale sign of CBS's deteriorating financial position under Tisch. Morita was warm to the idea, however, and urged me to accept the offer. "A new plant has yet to generate any profit," he noted, "and its

Announcing the acquisition of CBS's record business

book value is no more than the start-up investment. That's a bargain for Sony."

We ended up acquiring all of CBS's record and CD plants around the world, except one in the Republic of Korea. Morita and I shared doubts, however, about CBS's lasting viability in the music business. We mulled a plan to try to buy out CBS's stake in our joint venture and to thereby secure a wholly owned recorded music business. Yet the more we pondered, the more we became convinced that acquiring CBS's entire music business made more sense.

Our joint venture had earned its way initially on the strength of hits, like "The Sound of Silence," provided by CBS Records. But we had succeeded beyond our wildest dreams in cultivating Japanese singers, and homegrown talent had come to account for more than half of our revenues. That success emboldened us in our dealings with our joint venture partner.

CBS Records' CEO, Walter Yetnikoff, revealed that Tisch would likely be willing to let the music business go for $1.3 billion. We swallowed the bait and entered into negotiations to acquire the business in late 1986. Tisch, however, presented a different set of demands and an ever-fluctuating price for his record business at each meeting, and the negotiations foundered.

Tisch exhibited a renewed enthusiasm for divesting the music business after New York's Black Monday stock market crash of October 19, 1987. "Two billion dollars," he said, "and it's a done deal." Morita and I were all for the acquisition, but we faced powerful opposition inside Sony. Ibuka was noncommittal: "I don't know anything about the music business. The decision is for you to make on your own." We signed the agreement to acquire CBS Records in January 1988.

Three years after the acquisition, we renamed the subsidiary Sony Music Entertainment (Japan) and listed its shares on the Tokyo Stock Exchange. Divesting a mere 22% of its shares, Sony Music Entertainment raised the equivalent of $1.2 billion. That put the $2 billion purchase price in a new and eminently respectable perspective.

VII

Baptism by Fire in Hollywood

Sony's now-eminent position in Hollywood reflects the insight and
wisdom gleaned since its 1989 acquisition of Columbia Pictures. It
reflects, too, the company's continuing commitment to combining
content business and media business. Home video systems and movie
theater screens are the chief media for cinema content. Sony famously pioneered the market for home video. Even its legendary setback in
that market became a springboard for redoubled growth in the video
sector.

Losing the battle of the video formats—our Betamax and our rivals'
VHS—was a severe and humiliating blow. The stereotypical Japanese
accounts of the battle run something like this:

Sony's prideful preoccupation with technological originality proved
its undoing in competition with Matsushita Electric Industrial's assid-
uous consensus building. Matsushita and its subsidiary the Victor

Company of Japan, quintessentially Japanese companies, outdid Sony in eliciting support from numerous companies for their format. Sony's coldly U.S.-style management came up short in the battle for the hearts and minds of prospective Japanese partners.

The preceding interpretation holds immense appeal for Japanese who long to believe in the lasting pertinence of *japonesque* consensuality. It even contains a grain of truth, albeit highly exaggerated, as to how corporate cultures figured in the outcome of the video-format battle. For the record, Sony was and remains a conscientious partner to diverse counterparts, as well as an ever-fertile creator of innovative technologies. We were even a close partner with Matsushita and Victor in regard to product and manufacturing technology for videocassettes. Sony was thus a prime beneficiary, ironically, of the market surge that followed the consolidation around the VHS format. We received royalties from every manufacturer except Matsushita and Victor that produced VHS equipment.

Pity the negotiators from the Republic of Korea's Samsung Electronics. They spent a year working out a deal with Victor to secure technology to begin making and selling videotape recorders. No sooner had they finally inked the deal than they received a surprising message from their counterparts at Victor: "By the way, you ought to have a word with the folks at Sony on your way home. You'll need a license from them, too." I remember hearing that story from the nonplussed Samsung manager who visited Sony. That was the first he had heard of the three-way free cross-licensing arrangement between Matsushita, Victor, and our company.

We earned a great deal in technology-licensing fees from the VHS format—probably more than we would have earned from Betamax if it had become the industry standard. Our three-way cross-licensing arrangement was a highly efficient framework for defining patent coverage and for securing fees from licensees. None of this is to downplay the undeniably intense competition that took place between Sony and its VHS rivals. I would note, however, that I enjoyed good personal relations with Matsushita's legendary founder, Konosuke Matsushita, throughout the format battle. Matsushita was nearly half-a-century older than me, and he treated me like a favored grandchild. Based in Osaka, he frequently called when in Tokyo. We'd get together, and he'd pepper me with questions about the latest technologies. I'd call on him in Osaka, and he'd take me to the finest tearooms.

Licensing fees were a lucrative consolation prize from the video-format battle. An even bigger bonus, however, was our awakening to the importance of content assets. The rental video market burgeoned after the consolidation around the VHS format, and that called our attention to video content as a larger potential market for Sony than equipment.

Hospital detours

An unwelcome medical surprise and the loss of a beloved musical titan lay before me and the cinematic adventure that would redefine Sony's identity. In 1986, Morita became a vice-chairman at Japan's preeminent business federation, Keidanren. That federation is the central sounding board for Japanese big business, and Morita's accession to the ranks of vice-chairmen signified Sony's emergence as an accepted leader in Japan's business establishment. It also signified an increased workload for me in managing the company and in corporate diplomacy. The pressure took its toll in the form of a heart attack in March 1989.

Ignoring my physicians' frankest advice, I returned to work after a brief convalescence and performed without any handicap of note. I experienced sharp chest pain again, however, during a meeting at Sony Europe, in Cologne, in July 1989. That was the day after witnessing the passing of the incomparable Herbert von Karajan.

My wife and I had flown to Austria the day before with Sony America president Mickey Schulhof. Our plan was to visit von Karajan at his home in Salzburg. We arrived early, and I decided to stop at Sony's CD plant in the vicinity on the way. A woman met us at the airport, however, and conveyed a message from von Karajan that he would like us to come directly to his home.

Von Karajan's Italian butler, Francesco, greeted us with the news that the maestro was unwell and would receive us upstairs in his bedroom. Beside the prone maestro were the score of the Verdi opera *Un Ballo in Maschera*, which he was to conduct that year, and a Sony Walkman. Also in evidence were several airplane magazines.

The first question from von Karajan on seeing us was about what kind of aircraft we had flown in. We described the new-model Falcon in which we had flown, and a series of questions about the engine and other technical matters ensued. Von Karajan's wife, Eliette, interrupted us with the news that his physician had arrived. The maestro, however, turned the doctor away. Not even for the emperor of China, he declared, would he cut short his conversation with Mr. Ohga.

Von Karajan had been eager to let us know about his latest recordings. He sat up in the bed as he warmed to his subject but suddenly tired and asked for a glass of water. Mickey circled to the far side of the bed to fulfill the request. The maestro downed the glass of water gratefully, whereupon his head tilted sharply and the glass fell from his hand.

I dashed to summon Eliette. Sensing the moment of what was occurring, she shouted, "Herbert, Herbert!" as she charged into the room. The wife cradled the head of her now-motionless husband in her arms. Eliette then dashed off to try to recall the physician that she had just turned away, but he had left and was unavailable. The pursuit was, in any case, futile. Our beloved maestro was gone.

The loss of von Karajan before my eyes was a bigger shock than words could ever describe. More than a musical titan, he was a visionary who recognized before others the potential of digital recording. Even more, he was a friend and a mentor.

Life goes on, however, and life for me entailed more time in the hospital than anyone would choose if they had a choice. Fortunately, my time in the care of medical practitioners was always a time for conceiving new business ideas. Morita was visiting me in the hospital in 1989 when I broached the notion of acquiring a Hollywood studio. He scoffed at the idea initially, suggesting that I should concentrate on getting well, not on buying a Hollywood icon. But my proposal was visibly enticing to Morita, despite his pro forma resistance.

The idea of acquiring a movie studio had been floating around Sony for several years. Movies were a natural follow-up to our success in the music business. Cash was readily available, meanwhile, in the late years of Japan's economic bubble, and we at Sony had avoided the bubbly spending sprees on golf courses and hotels to which numerous Japanese companies had succumbed. Movie production was, in principle, a sound investment totally in conformance with our corporate strategy and culture. Morita soon decided that his hospitalized next in command was on to something, and he and I began examining the feasibility of a Hollywood acquisition in earnest.

The acquisition

Home videocasette recorders from Sony and other manufacturers had begun to transform Hollywood's business model, and the movie industry was in flux. We considered multiple potential acquisitions, but Columbia Pictures Entertainment was the best fit with our strategy. That's because we were looking for a large library of titles, as well as production capabilities.

Some studios, while excelling at producing hit movies, had sold off the secondary rights—such as the videocassette-distribution rights—to their films. Columbia Pictures owned a film library of nearly 3,000 titles. Those titles included such classics as *Lawrence of Arabia*, *Close*

Encounters of the Third Kind, and *Kramer vs. Kramer*, to name just a few. Equally appealing were Columbia's strong position in television production and its huge library of TV series. We were as interested in reaching consumers in their homes as in theaters, and Columbia's vault of content included 260 TV series and a total of 27,000 episodes.

Our earlier acquisition of CBS Records had been a friendly purchase of a close-knit organization with which we were intimately familiar. Columbia, we realized, would be far more difficult to assimilate into the Sony organization. Founded in 1924, Columbia was the fifth-largest Hollywood studio in the late 1980s, after Time Warner, Walt Disney, Paramount, and MCA/Universal, and it employed about 4,000 people. TriStar Pictures (then Tri-Star) was also a Columbia asset. Coca-Cola had owned Columbia since 1982, but the studio's ownership, management, and business structure had changed repeatedly in recent decades. Morale was low, meanwhile, on account of a recent dearth of hit movies.

Mickey Schulhof advised us to bring in a big-name producer from outside Columbia to run the company. Peter Guber, famed for such blockbusters as *Flashdance*, *Batman*, and *Rain Man*, emerged as the leading candidate. Securing the services of Guber would entail acquiring his movie-production unit, Guber-Peters Entertainment Company, as well as Columbia. So Guber and his partner, Jon Peters, became the joint heads of Columbia when we purchased the studio in 1989.

The nominal purchase price of Columbia was $3.4 billion. But the Columbia debt that we assumed and the cost of buying the Guber-

Peters company raised the total price to $4.8 billion. That struck a lot of people as a mind-boggling sum. Morita and I recognized, however, that movie and TV content were crucial to the future of Sony.

Usurping the soul of America

Epitomizing the rancor occasioned by our acquisition of Columbia was a *Newsweek* cover: "Japan Moves into Hollywood—Sony's $3.4 Billion Deal for Columbia Films." Adorning the cover was Columbia's iconic Statue of Liberty. The message was unmistakable: Sony was usurping the soul of America.

Our acquisition received soberer coverage from the *New York Times*, the *Los Angeles Times*, and other leading newspapers. We came in for renewed scrutiny a month later, however, when Japan's Mitsubishi Estate announced its acquisition of Rockefeller Center. Cultural frictions between the United States and Japan were flaming anew, and we were at the center of the blaze.

We took our case to the public. Morita in Japan and I in the United States held one media briefing after another. We explained that Sony was deepening its ties with American society through the Columbia acquisition. And we made steady progress in winning over the American public. Progress was slower, however, in coping with the fiscal burden incurred through the acquisition. Columbia's chief asset—its vault of movie titles and TV series—was illiquid, and our initial provisions to fund the investment would prove insufficient.

We renamed our studio Sony Pictures Entertainment. That was when we also renamed our music business Sony Music Entertainment. Sony Pictures got off to a good start. The studio released a series of successful films in its first two years, including the blockbusters *Terminator 2* and *Basic Instinct.* The hits, however, became fewer and farther between. Meanwhile, costs swelled as the studio tackled ever more extravagant productions. Sony Pictures' financial position deteriorated precariously, obliging us to undertake a sweeping restructuring of the studio. I decided that the restructuring should include replacing the studio heads.

Sony's fiscal year is from April to March, and we bit the Hollywood bullet in announcing our fiscal results for the interim period to September 1994. We wrote down the value of Sony Pictures and recorded a huge net loss. The write-down centered on "goodwill"—the excess of the acquisition price for assets over the book value of the assets acquired.

Goodwill arises commonly in connection with intangible assets, such as brand names, whose potential financial value is impossible to express on balance sheets. The price we paid for Columbia included a great deal of goodwill for the studio's library of movie and TV titles. But the studio's unprofitability and negative cash flow mandated a reduced valuation.

I was 64 years old when we took the write-down for Sony Pictures, and I had resolved to retire as president at 65. The write-down reduced the financial burden incurred on my watch and increased the managerial leeway for my successor. Our stock price fell, of course, after the announcement of the write-down. That drew the attention of the U.S. Securities and Exchange Commission, and I underwent two days of severe questioning about the write-down from the commission. The ultimate vindication for our decision, however, was the improvement in fiscal performance at Sony Pictures and at its parent company, Sony Corporation, that followed the restructuring.

VIII

Fun and Games

Sony Music Entertainment and Sony Pictures Entertainment exemplified the Sony strategy of complementing innovative strengths in electronic equipment with a strong presence in entertainment content. That strategy positioned Sony simultaneously at the cutting edge of high technology and in the vanguard of popular culture. And it impelled us to keep reinventing ourselves in anticipation of new possibilities, both technological and cultural. Once we began making good on the huge promise of our foothold in Hollywood, I identified the logical next step: computer games.

Ken Kutaragi, later to become the CEO of Sony Computer Entertainment, called my attention to the potential of computer games in the late 1980s. Nintendo was earning handsome profits with its Family Computer (marketed in the Americas, Europe, and Australia as the Nintendo Entertainment System), which was more toy than computer. Kutaragi, then a young engineer at Sony, was eager to develop a crucial component that Nintendo needed for its next-generation Family Computer, and he was fighting a lonely battle.

Ibuka and other Sony executives had soured on computer products after the commercial failure of our desktop calculator in the 1960s. The resistance to Kutaragi's initiative also reflected a perception that entering the game market would cheapen Sony's image. My experience in the record industry, however, had taught me the lucrative potential of the publishing business. And I recognized computer game consoles as a platform for a nascent business in publishing game titles. So I encouraged Kutaragi in his quest.

Computer byways

I should note that Iwama, my predecessor as Sony president, had remained more open-minded than his colleagues toward computers. He suggested that consumer computing was a natural part of our business, and work continued at Sony on some computer products. For example, we launched the world's smallest word processor, the Series 35, in the United States in 1980. We had developed that product at Iwama's urging to mark Sony's 35th anniversary.

Sony devoted immense effort to developing the Series 35 and even summoned Ibuka's son Makoto from IBM Japan to head the project. The 3.5-inch floppy disk, a famous Sony advance in personal computing, was among the technologies created for the word processor.

Other advanced functionality included the then-new capacity for data communications over telephone lines. The Series 35 was ahead of its time, though, and failed to meet our expectations in the marketplace.

Another Sony undertaking in personal computing was the MSX desktop computer. MSX was a software-hardware architecture standard proposed by Kazuhiko Nishi. A former Microsoft executive, Nishi was the founder of ASCII Corporation, which served for a time as Microsoft's sales agency for the Far East. He enlisted Microsoft, Matsushita, Philips, Sharp, Yamaha, and several other equipment makers and software developers in the MSX project.

Morita's son Masao initiated the Sony MSX project at Nishi's invitation. Equipped with an eight-bit microprocessor, our MSX went on the market in 1983. The Sony MSX was a technological success, but its product life proved short. Most of the MSX owners used the computer as a game console, and the 1983 launch of the MSX coincided fatefully with the launch of Nintendo's Family Computer.

Sony also participated in a project promoted by Japan's Ministry of International Trade and Industry (now the Ministry of Economy, Trade and Industry) to develop a workstation based on a 32-bit microprocessor. We launched our 32-bit workstation in 1987 as the NEWS, and it fulfilled the ministry's development criteria admirably. Sony lacked sufficient capabilities in overall system planning, however, to compete with specialized computer manufacturers, and our workstation failed to take hold in the marketplace. Yet the technology and know-how accumulated in the NEWS project later spawned our highly successful Vaio line of laptop computers.

Nintendo's guile

In the late 1980s, Kutaragi took the initiative in developing business in supplying Nintendo with pulse code modulation (PCM) sound synthesizers for the Family Computer. And he wanted to supply Sony-developed CD-ROM drives for the next-generation Family Computer, the Super Family Computer (Super Nintendo Entertainment System), which was then under development.

I gave Kutaragi the go-ahead to negotiate a deal with Nintendo, and I signed an agreement with Nintendo's then-president Hiroshi Yamauchi to formalize our collaboration. That was in January 1990, when the development work on the Super Family Computer was well under way. In advance of announcing our collaboration publicly, Kutaragi and I prepared to pay a courtesy call at Nintendo's Kyoto headquarters in the company of Nobuyuki Idei, Kutaragi's boss at the time and later my successor as Sony president. Nintendo, however, pulled the rug out from under our impending partnership. It unveiled the specifications for the Super Family Computer at the U.S. Consumer Electronics Show in June 1991, and those specifications called for using a Philips Compact Disc Interactive (CD-i) device instead of the Sony CD-ROM drive.

Dumbfounded, we inquired into the reason for Nintendo's astounding change of heart. The answer only heightened our incredulity: Yamauchi denied having any recollection of having signed the agreement with Sony. What we learned later was that Yamauchi's son-in-law, then the head of Nintendo's U.S. operations, had apparently nixed the deal. The son-in-law, Minoru Arakawa, had witnessed firsthand the stunning growth in U.S. sales of CD-ROM drives and disks. Arakawa knew that Sony had built a strong position in CD-ROM products. And he apparently feared that Sony would get the better of Nintendo in a collaboration.

The people at Nintendo ultimately conceded that the agreement with Sony was valid. They said that we were welcome to produce Family Computer–compatible game consoles based on CD-ROMs. Nintendo, however, would use a different standard for the game media in its consoles. I regarded the whole affair as a humiliation for Sony, and I asked Kutaragi and his team if they thought we should go ahead with our plans for producing Nintendo-compatible consoles. They responded with a resounding "No." The market for CD-ROM–based consoles would never take off, they reasoned, without Nintendo's participation. Nintendo had rendered the joint-development agreement with Sony worthless and had sabotaged Kutaragi's carefully conceived scenario for game business.

In the eyes of those at Sony who had argued against entering the game business, the setback was our comeuppance. I felt responsible for the project, having given the go-ahead, and I was unwilling to simply abandon the undertaking. Kutaragi and his team, meanwhile, were unbowed in their determination to build a game-console business for Sony.

Shigeo Maruyama was cultivating a position in game software at Sony Music Entertainment, and I asked him to find a place for Kutaragi and some of his engineers at his headquarters. Sony Music

Entertainment proved the perfect redoubt for the Kutaragi team. Maruyama had mastered the arcane arts of the music business, and he imparted his learning to his new charges. Kutaragi and his engineers thus became direct heirs to the content-business tradition that we had fostered in our music and movie operations. I am confident that their subsequent success benefited hugely from what they absorbed at Sony Music Entertainment and that they never would have achieved anything comparable if they had been working inside the parent-company organization.

We also continued talking with Nintendo to see if we couldn't work out some kind of compromise, but the talks proved fruitless. That left us with the stark choice of walking away from the game-console market or creating a business there from scratch. All of Sony's senior executives except me turned against the project. Even I had all but abandoned hope when we summoned Kutaragi one day in July 1992 to provide an accounting. Defiant as ever, Kutaragi faced the assembled executives and issued a challenge. Were we really prepared, he asked, to simply give up? Were we willing, he continued, to let Sony become a laughingstock?

On questioning, Kutaragi revealed that his team had nearly completed a prototype game console. The machine contained a CD-ROM drive and flaunted an awesome range of computer graphics. It would use a high-performance semiconductor device to be developed especially for the machine. The other executives present remained skeptical. But I was unable to restrain myself in my excitement at the news. Pounding the table, I blurted out in English, "Do it!"

The PlayStation

Our first PlayStations hit the store shelves just in time for the Christmas season in 1994. It was the launch of a product that would do more than any other to fortify our bottom line. And it came just a month after we announced the massive write-down of our Hollywood investment. The name PlayStation was a play on the word "workstation." It was the name we had chosen for what was to have been our Nintendo-compatible game console, and we liked the name so much that we retained it despite the unpleasant history.

Sales of Sony PlayStations and Sony game software for the consoles reached ¥1 trillion in 2002, and sales of PlayStation game software by third-party developers totaled even more. The PlayStation, in other words, had become a ¥2 trillion-plus market. We had sold more than 95 million PlayStation consoles. No other consumer electronics product in history had burgeoned into such a huge market in just eight years.

The first-generation PlayStation in the marketplace

Besides Kutaragi, two individuals who deserve special mention in regard to the PlayStation project are Tamotsu Iba and Teruhisa Tokunaka. Both were executives in our financial operations. Iba later became the chairman of Sony Computer Entertainment, and Tokunaka—recalled from the United States to help with the PlayStation project—later became Sony's chief financial officer. Both men worked wonders in securing the necessary funding for the project and in shaping a workable business plan.

Two factors figured decisively in the success of the PlayStation: our choice of CD-ROMs for the game software and our adoption of a two-handed grip for the game controller. CD-ROMs, unlike the semiconductor ROM chips that we also considered, allow for writing data easily and affordably. That opened the market for PlayStation titles to small game developers, as well as to larger and well-heeled developers. It helped ensure a large range of PlayStation titles early on and thereby stimulated demand greatly.

Our grip controller, meanwhile, was a departure from the traditional push-button controllers. Its subsequent popularity notwithstanding, the controller almost failed to earn a place in the final product. Some of our game software development people complained that the controller was too different from Nintendo's. They argued that the unfamiliar design would put off customers and hurt sales.

Kutaragi and the PlayStation's chief designer, Teiyu Goto, took the objections seriously—so seriously that they brought a prototype for a more-conventional controller to my office and asked for my approval to use it instead of the two-handed grip. I reminded them that we had set out to create a completely new game platform, and I insisted that the controller should be new, too. Tossing the prototype onto my desk, I instructed Kutaragi and Goto to use the grip-type controller that they had shown me earlier.

The configuration of our controller was similar to the yoke (steering wheel) in an aircraft, and it was easy for users to hold and manipulate while assuming any posture. Nintendo's subsequent adoption of a grip configuration affirmed the wisdom of our choice.

Epilogue: Originality

A commitment to doing things "our own way" has shaped Sony's growth and development since the company's beginning. I inherited that commitment and nurtured it carefully during my years at Sony, and I passed that commitment on to my successors. Morita was the best-known personification of Sony's creative nonconformity, but Ibuka, Iwama, and the company's other leaders have each furthered the Sony tradition of originality.

Readers might be surprised to learn that the Walkman, Morita's most-famous innovation, originated not with him but with Ibuka. One day, Ibuka came to me and said he wanted to be able to listen to his favorite music while traveling on airliners. He asked me to provide him with a miniature stereo tape player. We modified our newest cassette tape player, equipped it with headphones, and presented the compact unit to Ibuka. One problem with the tape player was the special batteries we had employed to minimize the size. Ibuka was unable to buy replacement batteries overseas. He was delighted with the tape player, nonetheless, and showed it to Morita on his return.

Morita tried the tape player and declared instantly that it had commercial potential. In a momentous misjudgment, I was utterly dismissive of the gadget. The little gadget contained no genuinely new technology and lacked even a recording function. I simply couldn't imagine who would ever want to own one.

The name Walkman owes its global currency to an insight by Morita's wife, Yoshiko. Morita regarded that name as a Japanese perversion of English and wanted to call the product Sound About in markets outside Japan. Yoshiko suggested, however, that Walkman was a perfectly good name and that, anyway, the product deserved a unified global identity. Fortunately, she was sufficiently persuasive.

Succession

Ibuka served as the president of Sony for 21 years. Morita, however, turned over the helm to Iwama after only 5 years in the post, though he retained the title of CEO for another 13 years. Iwama was president for a mere 6 years. In retaining the presidency for 12 years, I probably overstayed my welcome. I was only 52, however, when I succeeded Iwama in 1982, so I was hardly a gerontocrat.

Our operations became too vast and complex during my years as president for any single individual to micromanage from the top. We

Naming Nobuyuki Idei to succeed the author as president

therefore revamped our management structure in 1994 and reposi-
tioned our eight principal businesses as virtual companies, each with
its own CEO. Along with streamlining management, that allowed me
to evaluate the management capabilities of eight candidates for the
presidency of Sony. I planned to retire in January 1995, when I would
turn 65, and the timing was right to choose a successor. The issue of
succession gained increased urgency in late December. That was when
Morita, then our chairman, collapsed with a cerebral hemorrhage
while playing tennis.

I had always discussed important decisions with Morita, and I had
assumed that he would participate in choosing my successor. Morita's
incapacitation left me alone at the top, and that was the loneliest I had
felt in my life.

Nobuyuki Idei soon emerged as the best-qualified candidate. He
had performed impressively in setting up our French subsidiary.
Although not an engineer by training, he had an excellent command
of the technological aspects of our business. And he possessed the most

important trait for a Sony leader: a strong and visible commitment to maximizing the brand value of the Sony name. I had never worked with Idei directly on a daily basis, but I knew enough to recognize that he was the best choice for president. Seven years younger than me, he was entering his prime as an executive.

I had a brief meeting with Idei as my 65th birthday approached and explained that I wanted him to succeed me as president. He was about to leave on a business trip and asked for some time to consider the offer before giving me his answer. That was only fair and natural, and I encouraged him to give the matter careful thought. I assumed, of course, that Idei would accept the position, and I was startled at the reply that he sent back during his trip. He stated that he was the wrong person for the job and asked me to reconsider.

Idei's becoming president would mean leapfrogging 14 more-senior executives. I was confident in my judgment, however, and stood by my decision. Idei's exemplary performance as president more than justified my decision. He remained unhappy with me, however, for a crucial transgression: I never responded to his initial refusal.

Norio Ohga and Sony Over the Years

Year	Age	Ohga	Sony
1930		Born in Shizuoka Prefecture	
1946			Established by Masaru Ibuka and Akio Morita as Tokyo Tsushin Kogyo in Tokyo's Nihombashi district
1947			Moves factory to Tokyo's Shinagawa district
1949	19	Graduates from high school; enters Tokyo National University of Fine Arts and Music	
1950			Launches Japan's first tape recorder
1953	23	Graduates from university; becomes contract employee of Tokyo Tsushin Kogyo; performs as soloist with NHK Symphony Orchestra	
1954	24	Completes graduate studies at Tokyo National University of Fine Arts and Music; begins musical studies in Munich	
1955	25	Transfers to Berlin University of the Arts	Lists shares on over-the-counter market; launches Japan's first transistor radio
1957	27	Graduates from Berlin University of the Arts; returns to Japan; marries	
1958			Changes name to Sony; lists shares on Tokyo Stock Exchange
1959	29	Becomes full-time employee at Sony, responsible initially for production of tape recorders for radio stations	
1960			Establishes Sony Corporation of America; launches world's first nonprojection-type all-transistor television
1961	31	Assumes responsibility for advertising	Becomes first Japanese company to issue equity (American depositary receipts) in United States
1963			Launches world's first all-transistor compact videotape recorder
1964	34	Becomes member of Sony's board of directors	
1965			Launches world's first home videotape recorder
1966			Signs cross-licensing agreement with Philips in regard to magnetic recording and reproduction technology
1968	38	Becomes senior managing director at CBS/Sony Records	Establishes CBS/Sony Records as joint venture with CBS; launches first Trinitron color television model
1970	40	Becomes president of CBS/Sony Records	Lists shares on New York Stock Exchange
1971			Ibuka becomes chairman and Morita president

Year	Age	Ohga	Sony
1972	42	Becomes managing director at Sony	
1974	44	Becomes senior managing director at Sony	Opens television plant in United Kingdom
1975			Launches Betamax home videotape recorder
1976	46	Becomes executive deputy president at Sony	Morita becomes chairman and Kazuo Iwama president
1979			Launches Walkman; establishes Sony Prudential Life Insurance (now Sony Life) as joint venture with Prudential Insurance Company of America
1980	50	Becomes chairman of CBS/Sony	
1982	52	Becomes Sony's president and chief operating officer	Launches CD player; Iwama passes away
1985			Launches charge-coupled device (CCD) 8 mm video camera
1986			Establishes Sony Europe in Germany
1987			Launches computer workstation
1988			Acquires CBS's music business
1989	59	Becomes Sony's chief executive officer	Acquires Columbia Pictures Entertainment
1991			Renames music business Sony Music Entertainment and movie business Sony Pictures Entertainment
1992			Launches MiniDisc system
1993			Establishes Sony Computer Entertainment
1994			Reorganizes operations as semiautonomous virtual companies; Morita becomes honorary chairman; launches PlayStation
1995	65	Becomes chairman, retaining title of chief executive officer	Nobuyuki Idei becomes president
1996			Marks 50th anniversary of founding
1997			Ibuka passes away
1999	69	Becomes president of Tokyo Philharmonic Orchestra	Idei becomes Sony's chief executive officer; Morita passes away
2000	70	Becomes chairman of Sony's board of directors	Idei becomes executive chairman of Sony, retaining title of chief executive oficer; Kunitake Ando becomes president and chief operating officer
2003	73	Retires from Sony's board of directors and becomes company's honorary chairman	
2006	76	Becomes senior advisor to Sony	

Index

119

charge-coupled device. *See* CCD
Chromatron, 34
color television, 32; Ibuka and technology
for, 33
Columbia Group, 50; Nippon Columbia
and, 51
Columbia Pictures Entertainment, ix, x,
96; acquisition of, 91; film library of, 96;
purchase price of, 97–98; television
strength of, 97; unprofitability of, xiv
compact cassette tape recorder, xiii
compact disc. *See* CD
Compact Disc (CD) Digital Audio
System, 45, 70; Iwama and, 70
content and hardware, x, xiv–xv
content and media businesses, 91
content assets, 93
content-business tradition, 106
content versus manufacturing businesses,
xvi, xvii
corporate governance: as hybrid, xviii;
globalization and, xviii
corporate identity, xi, 17, 29
corporate plane, 78–79
corporate planning, 67
cross-licensing agreement, 92, 93
cultural frictions, 98

D

data communications, 103
Dekker, Wisse, 39, 40, 41
design: annual trip for, 29; competitions
in, 28; fostering camaraderie in, 28–29
Digital Audio Disk (DAD) Conference, 45
diverse operations, xvi, xvii

E

electronic components: earnings value of,
xv–xvi; third-party customers and, xvi
entertainment business: content side of, x;
volatility of, xv, xvi
error-correction technology, 43
Esaki, Leona, 70

F

finances, xv
floppy disk, 102

G

Germany, 4–5, 9
Godzilla, ix
Goto, Teiyu, 108
Grundig, Max, 39

H

heart attack, 94
helicopter crash, 80–81
Hollywood, 91, 95, 96
home video pioneers, 91
Honda Motor, 9
Honda, Soichiro, 9–10
human resources, flexibility of, xviii–xix

I

Iba, Tamotsu, 108
Ibuka, Masaru, xvi, xvii, 1, 4, 39, 63;
appeal of, 2, 3–4; as go-between, 15; as
technological genius, 64; Chromatron
and, 34; computer decision of, 69;
German trip of, 12; management style
of, 71; passion evinced by, xix; Sony
originality and, 111; steel nerves of, 80;
transistors and, 64
Idei, Nobuyuki, 104, 113
in-house companies, 113; managerial
responsibility for, xviii; useful system
of, xvii
innovation pioneer, xix
Iwama, Kazuo: as seminal force, 71; CCDs
and, 66; choosing successor to, 73; computers and, 102; funeral for, 73;
gravesite visit and, 68; Ibuka and Morita
and, 63–64; Iwama Reports and, 65;
joins company, 64; originality and, 111;
passing of, 48, 67–68; R&D team built
by, 70; semiconductors and, 63, 70; suc-
ceeds Morita, 67